ENDORSEMENTS

My first introduction to Chris was through his articles in the local newspaper. I looked forward with anticipation to each topic addressed, nodding my head while reading. It felt like he was personally addressing me, relaying meaningful stories, sharing famous quotes, and presenting basic wisdom. After working on a series of podcasts with Chris centered on the eight facets of life, it was evident this Christian holds a true passion for helping others grow and become their very best. His message is simple and each reader can pull out something of personal value within the pages. Chris's book is designed to make you think about your beliefs, your goals, and your life. Please accept his invitation to read, ponder, and uncover what speaks to you. -**Deborah Ellis, Educational Consultant**

Chris Conley has written a book I believe everyone can relate to and benefit from regardless of the stage of life you find yourself in. We all have God-given potential. Sadly, not many of us fulfill ours. This is a book you will find difficult to put down. The stories and illustrations make it compelling and reader friendly. It is likely to become a handbook of sorts for navigating the critical aspects of a life well-lived. Each section is like having a conversation with a trusted friend. As a holistic health coach, I address spirit, soul and body with all my clients because health is a wholeness issue and all aspects must be addressed. This is exactly what Chris has done here. He shares from his personal experience as well as from what he's learned through the years from others. He has provided resources as well as powerful illustrations that empower the reader to take the next step and begin incorporating those tips instead of leaving them on the page. -**Ann Musico, Holistic Health Coach and author of Today is Still the Day**

The engaging stories made me laugh and cry. And the principles woven in reminded me of the most important practices for living fully alive and finishing strong. -**Dan Miller, author of 48 Days to the Work You Love, and host of the 48 Days Podcast**

Sadly, there are too many successful adults who are feeling lost, burdened, confused, and unsure. In reality, they have not yet realized the true meaning of success. Author Chris Conley uses is own experiences, coupled with research and education to offer 8 essential character traits and personal growth opportunities, which, when applied properly, can be the essential tools to mold an individual in the direction God always intended.

This easy to read book includes key takeaways and encouraging tips, designed to assist the reader in applying the information into everyday life.

Chris is direct, but kind in his approach. I highly recommend. -**Jennifer Beck, Anchor, Reporter, Producer, Director of Marketing, WTLW TV-44**

Honored to be listed as one of the top 5 personal development experts in the world. Jon Gordon, 11x best-selling author of the Energy Bus and The Carpenter -**Jon Gordon**

Touching Lives with Dr. James Merritt is humbled to be recognized as a top 5 faith-based resource. We give all glory to God for such recognition. -**James Merritt**

The 8 Facets of Life

Everyone Ends up Somewhere -Make Sure You End up Somewhere on Purpose

The 8 Facets of Life

Everyone Ends up Somewhere -Make Sure You End up Somewhere on Purpose

CHRIS CONLEY

Copyright 2021 © by Chris Conley

All rights reserved. No part of this book may be reproduced or transmitted by any form or by any means, electronic or mechanical, including photocopying and recording, or by any information storage and retrieval system, without permission in writing from author and publisher.

Unless noted, all Bible quotations are from the
New Living Translation® Bible, copyright © 2003, 2004.
Used by permission by Tyndale House Foundation. All rights reserved

Printed in the United States of America
2021 First Edition

Subject Index:
Conley, Chris
The 8 Facets of Life -Everyone Ends up Somewhere -Make Sure You End up Somewhere on Purpose
1. Christian 2. Inspirational 3. Personal Growth 4. Family Relationships

Paperback ISBN: 978-1-64746-833-0
Hardback ISBN: 978-1-64746-834-7
Ebook: 978-1-64746-835-4
LCCN: 2021911609

Author Academy Elite, Powell OH

DEDICATION

I would like to dedicate this book to the next generation, especially my grandchildren.

I believe the advice and principles laid out on these pages will make all the difference you need.

They are easy to do, but so simple, they can often be neglected.

Knowledge is powerful, but only if acted upon.

I would also like to dedicate this book to my wife. She's been my encourager throughout life. I owe her much.

Lastly to my daughter-in-law, Julie. She helped me complete this project when I was stuck. Her insight and advice was invaluable.

CONTENTS

Foreword xi
Introduction xiii
Chapter 1 Personal Development 1
Chapter 2 Family 20
Chapter 3 Relationships 57
Chapter 4 Health 70
Chapter 5 Career 86
Chapter 6 Finance 108
Chapter 7 Fun / Joy 135
Chapter 8 Faith 145
Conclusion 171
Philosophy 175
About the Author 179

FOREWORD

I am honored to be asked to write the forward to the book; *The 8 Facets of Life*. I've known Chris for a few years and the thing that stands out to me about him is his genuine interest in attempting to help others. I've seen him hand out books that he has read to others as well as teaching our men's group on occasions.

As a fellow youth coach, we've shared stories about the high's you experience in helping others reach their potential.

I believe you will fast track your personal development growth by reading the following pages and taking the advice before you. I wish I had this information much earlier in my life, but regardless of your age it's time to take the initiative and make yourself all you can be for yourself and those that depend on you.

I've heard Chris say before, even the wisest man who ever lived, Solomon, in writing his advice to the world, included much of what others input he'd learned. That's exactly what Chris has attempted to do as well. Use his knowledge and experience as well as other's experiences, and finally what he's read or heard told.

None of us have all the answers. That's why we need to stay connected as the vine is to the branch.

        - **Ryan Miller, Kenton Middle School teacher and friend of the author**

INTRODUCTION

When I was working, I used to be on the road by 4:30 am. One particular day the fog was making the drive extremely difficult. Combine fog with darkness and no other traffic and you can see how I could quickly lose track of my current location.

I think that's similar to how many of us live our lives. We're headed somewhere but not sure it's the right place.

Pursuing your potential means driving in the dark.

It would have been easier had there been other cars on the road. Additional headlights and tail lights could have helped me see the road. But there wasn't a lot of traffic. Likewise, there won't be a lot of traffic when you begin to pursue your potential. There will be people telling you to stay where you are. They will discourage your ambition. You might have to travel a lonely road. That's OK. The road to significance is less congested than the road to mediocrity.

Dark. Dense fog. Unfamiliarity.

Those were the ingredients for a very stressful drive. The road was hilly and curvy. It was the time of year when deer wander into the road with no warning. I knew the destination very well—work. But seeing the path was nearly impossible.

Just 5 minutes into my drive I crossed a major highway and my vehicle seemed to go air born, if just slightly, as I ran the stop sign. I realized where I was and realized the danger. I turned around and got on the highway and thought to turn on my GPS. The dot on the screen represented my location. I was then able to see what to expect next. Because I couldn't see where I was going, I had to trust the instruments. "It's going to bend to the right and then back to the left." Those were reassuring instructions in the midst of uncertainty. I made it to work safely and that ordeal has stayed with me since.

There are a few lessons I think we all can learn from my driving experience.

Pursuing your potential means driving in the fog.

Once I started driving, I only had two choices. I could stop and wait for the fog to clear or keep moving and eventually drive out of the fog. Waiting it out wasn't an option if I would make it there on time, so I had to rely on my GPS to "see" what was ahead. Moving forward might be like driving in the fog for you as well. Don't stop. Let those who love you help you see the road ahead. That's the only way to make it to the destination.

Unfamiliarity is the landscape of achievement.

To get where you've never been before, you will have to travel unfamiliar roads. If you stick to the familiar paths, you'll only arrive at familiar destinations.

Do you want the remainder of your life to be a time you reach levels of success you've not yet experienced? If so, brace yourself for what's ahead. There won't be much traffic. The fog might be thicker than you've ever seen. Unfamiliarity will try to convince you to stick to what you've always done. Keep moving! Don't let your past determine the boundaries for your future.

The rest of your life can be different.

It can be a repeat of the past.

Which version do you want?

In the book *The Eight Facets of Life* author Chris Conley will lead you on a journey. The journey of life. I believe there are eight key components that make up our life. While everyone would agree with these once reading, sadly we might not understand the impact we're having in these various areas of our life. That is unless we take the time to examine them. I

Introduction

stumbled onto this a few years ago and realized with a different mindset, life could possibly be lived more meaningful. No guarantees, but it could or should be much better once reading this book, heeding the advice that applies to you and applying some of the tips.

I believe that the priority we place on each of these facets can and most likely will change over time. It did in my life and probably will in yours as well. The book is laid out in a format that can be read as many other books, front to back, highlight the key points that speak to you for later reference. Or perhaps you'll skip a chapter on finance because you are already a millionaire and couldn't possibly learn anything new on that subject. Or I would suggest reading it all with your highlights and dog-eared pages, then referring back to certain chapters if and when a particular aspect of your life isn't all it could be.

My hope is there is enough good information that the time spent will be well worth it. Many of these lessons I've learned after I already made the mistake. Sometimes that's the best way to learn but I've always liked the quote, "learn from others mistakes, because you'll never live long enough to make them all yourself." That certainly makes sense.

Many of these tips were learned the hard way, through experience. Some are learned from observation, some learned from reading either a newsletter, blog or book. Lastly from hearing, be it a friend or speaker. I have always enjoyed learning new things, especially things I could apply to my life, be it career, as a parent, husband, or any of the other facets of life.

I trust you will enjoy it as well. If you have any comments after reading, please visit the facebook page The Eight facets of Life. I would appreciate your thoughts or feedback.

In the intro I wrote about pursuing your potential. I shared my experience of driving in the fog and the similarities of how we live our lives. My hope was to encourage readers to make plans for self-improvement.

Many people have these thoughts, especially around the first of the year. We make resolutions that typically fail. I've always looked forward to Jan 1st as I do to the 1st of any month. It seems like a fresh start. I like to ask myself the question(s) what could I be doing differently, or what should I be doing differently in order to be better myself? I think that's a worthwhile goal for all of us.

I've always been a goal setter, maybe not formally, maybe I'm more of a dreamer.

You see, I've heard the experts say a goal that's not written is just a dream. That 80% of all New Year's resolutions fail in the first month. I think that's why many people say, why bother!

However, I think everyone wants to be better. The question may be where to start? Or how to get started? I'd like to go in depth with what's made me ponder these questions and why I think you should as well.

While I was working, salespeople would bring in many things around Christmastime as a thank you for doing business. Items such as food and candy as well as calendars and planners.

One year I received a planner. I'd received planners before and always looked forward to seeing this year's model. I've always enjoyed admiring the cover, glossy with a nice picture, or one with a nice leather feel. More important than that was the inside. Most would have an inspirational quote with each month. I'd read them and think about the meaning behind the meaning. Then there were all the incidentals. The dates to remember, notes, contacts etc. Every year I'd tell myself, this is the year I'll be more organized than ever.

This planner however had a page that was unlike anything I'd ever seen. It started with personal information, the months with some inspiring quotes, some pages for advance

Introduction

planning, contact information, time zones and zip codes etc. One page however had a page labeled "goals". Goals weren't new to me; I'd been doing work or career goals all my working days. I'd also always considered personal goals around this time of year like health or weight loss, and finance. This page of goals however went much deeper.

They listed 9 in total and included career, education, faith, family, financial, fitness, health, relationships, and other. As I pondered these a thought came to me, if there were areas of my life that were important, then why wouldn't I make a goal to improve! Most people myself included would say family is important, but how many of us make a family goal? The same could be said for faith, but how many faith goals are made?

I could go on and on because different people are motivated by different aspects of life. Yet most of us go through life like we're driving through the fog I mentioned. This new concept got me thinking and more importantly evaluating or reflecting on my life. As I read the list again, I wondered, are these all the key areas of our life or was something missing?

Career made sense and needed no editing. Education sounded too formal to me, like a diploma or end of a course. I liked the heading personal development better because to me it says, lifelong learning. Faith was fine, as was family and financial. Fitness and health seemed like they could be combined into just health. My logic was you can't have health without some form of fitness. Relationships sounded ok although I considered combining them with family into social. However, the longer I thought about it I concluded for most people there is a difference between family and relationships so I kept them both. Lastly "other" I didn't care for. Other is just a catch all. I thought about my own life and asked what would go here. I came up with hobbies etc. At first, I settled on lifestyle but later decided to call the final category fun. With that I had eight components that make up life.

I've since called this *The Eight Facets of Life*.

Each chapter I'll write on a different facet of life. Beginning with personal development, then moving to family, relationships, health, career, finance, fun, and finally faith.

I'll share stories, quotes, tips etc on each and attempt to give you material or resources to improve yourself. The last chapter I'll wrap things up with a summary, and what next.

I'll share my thoughts on the subject, not to say I've got it all figured out, but rather to get you thinking about your own life, where you can improve, do you need to improve, and hopefully how to get there.

I hope you'll read each chapter, digest it, then decide, does this apply to me? Is there a growth opportunity for me as well? If not, great, wait for the next chapter. If so however I'll have some suggestions where you might be able to turn for help. In addition, there may be readers who have better suggestions than I. If that's the case I'd encourage you to join the Facebook group and share your opinions there.

I've worked on this for over 25 years. Some areas I'm naturally stronger than others. Some come easy while others not so easy, no doubt to you as well.

In summary I'll share all I've learned with you and give you the opportunity to share your thoughts and suggestions.

I believe there is something here for everyone. Whether you are a long-time personal development expert, or if you're brand new to the experience, this can accelerate your growth by taking years off the learning curve.

Looking forward to all that's ahead and seeing past the fog of mediocrity

CHAPTER 1

PERSONAL DEVELOPMENT

A person who won't read has no advantage over a person who can't read.

What is it?

Some people would refer to this title as education but to me that sounds too formal. When I think of education it sounds like it has an ending, such as when a diploma is received. Personal development on the other hand is a life-long never-ending process.

It could be said that personal development is everything you learn after your formal schooling is complete. Some of it comes to us by experience. Sometimes it's from mistakes made. Although painful many times these are the best lessons. Another way to learn is from other people's mistakes. Whether it's from their telling, your observation, or you reading about it, this is definitely a less painful way to learn.

Why is it important?

In my design of *The Eight Facets of Life*, I list personal development at the top. Not because it's the most important, but in my mind, it probably affects the other seven more than any other. It affects them as in a ripple effect. For example, if I read a book on how to have a better marriage, it would be helping my personal development but also my family. If

I took a course to be a better leader in my work, it helps my personal development but also my career. The same could be said for my finances, relationships, health, faith or fun. When I develop myself beyond my current capabilities there is a ripple effect that touches multiple other areas.

It's been said we can improve ourselves by the books we read or the people we are around. It's what we allow into our minds. I'll go into this more in the final chapter under the heading of Philosophy. For now, though, please consider taking the time to read books, attend seminars, etc. There is a suggested book list at the end of this chapter.

Many people will say I just don't have the time or can't make the time for personal development at this stage of my life. As valid as this may be, it's still a necessity. Carve out thirty minutes a day, be it first thing in the morning or before going to bed. It could be reading during your lunch break, listening to a podcast while getting ready for the day, or any other time you can find. If you can't commit to thirty, start with ten minutes and build up to thirty. The important thing is to start.

Another suggestion is to be sure to always have something--a trade magazine, a book, headphones for listening to an audiobook or podcast-- with you so that you can be productive in downtime. For example, when going to an appointment you'll often arrive early and have several minutes to wait. Use that time to learn something new! Zig Ziglar, a globally known motivational speaker for over forty years, suggests turning your vehicle into "Automobile University." His coined phrase, "You don't just sit there to get there," urges people to use traveling as a time to expand knowledge on a topic by listening to audiobooks, speeches, podcasts, etc.

Personal Development

* * *

I enjoy daily devotions in the morning, I feel that this sets my day up for success with something inspirational versus any type of news. By all means stay away from newspapers, television, radio etc. especially first thing in the morning. You don't need tragedy anytime, really, but especially not after a good night's sleep. When you think about it, what are you going to do about a robbery on the other end of town along with everything else that's reported? I've also committed to thirty minutes of reading prior to going to bed for the night. You'd be surprised by getting into this habit how much better you'll sleep, and I find myself many times dreaming about something I've read. I guess that makes sense as it was the last thing I've thought about.

I'd like to share a story that brings to life why we need personal development. No doubt most people have flown before. The flight attendant, when presenting general and emergency directions, explains that if the plane loses cabin pressure, the oxygen masks will drop from the ceiling. When this happens, passengers should be sure to secure their own before helping others.

Imagine you are traveling with your child or grandchild. You may think, *they are my number one priority. I'll certainly help them first.* But what if during the commotion you fail to secure theirs and pass out. No one is helped in that circumstance. You both may perish. Therefore, you must first take care of yourself before you can be of any value to anyone else.

This concept makes all the sense in the world to me. If I'm not around I can do no earthly good to anyone. Throughout my life I've attempted to share things I've learned with others, sometimes with results, and yet many times the person would have no interest. It can be frustrating to say the least, but I've always bought into the fact that it is our responsibility to plant the seed. In time the idea may grow into results.

The following sums personal development up best: *When I was young, I wanted to change the world. When I saw I couldn't change the world, I tried to change my country. When I saw I couldn't change my country, I tried to change my town. When I saw I couldn't change my town, I tried to change my family. When I saw I couldn't, I realized if I'd changed myself, I'd have influenced my family, they would have influenced our town, and our town would have influenced our country, and our country would have influenced the world* (an unknown Monk).

Help others, help yourself. A rising tide floats all ships.

I got hooked on personal development years ago reading Zig Ziglar newsletters. Sometime after that I saw an advertisement for a Peter Lowe *Get Motivated* Conference. The price was only $49, and I persuaded my employer to send me and a small group of my colleagues. I explained to the group prior to going that this wasn't just a day away from work, but that we should go there with the purpose to learn. I planned to take notes and suggested they should as well. I informed them that the day following the conference we would debrief and share our thoughts.

The general consensus was that the day was well worth it. Overall, the speakers were very inspiring. Naturally some better than others, but all were worth hearing. I think we tend to get out of something in similar proportions to what effort we put out. If I expect to get nothing of value from a speaker, chances are pretty good I won't. Even if there is valuable content to be heard, because I've tuned them out, nothing comes from the experience. On the other hand, if my intentions are to come away with something new, there is a very good chance that I will.

Help others, help yourself

A story is told of a mountain climber who was taken by a surprise snowstorm. He lost his way and realized he needed to find shelter fast or else face frostbite, and possible death. In his wandering he literally tripped over another man who was almost frozen. He had to decide to save himself or try to help the man. He knelt beside the man and began to massage the man's legs and arms. After several minutes he helped the fellow hiker to his feet and together they found help. The hiker was later told by helping another he'd helped himself. The numbness that had stricken him vanished while he massaged the strangers body. His heightened activity had enhanced his circulation and brought warmth to his own hands and feet. This is an example of trying to save yourself, yet realizing life is about others, and while helping them, we are also helping ourselves.

Isn't it ironic that when we lose sight of ourselves and focus on someone else and their predicament, we can many times solve our own problems?

We never stop learning. The more we learn, the more we can help ourselves and eventually others.

A concept I first heard from Jim Rohn--businessman, author, and speaker who I'll reference again in the chapter on career--*Work harder on yourself than you do on your job*. Let that sink in. It's not saying don't work hard on your job... just work harder on yourself.

You should always give your best effort on your job. The key is what you do with your discretionary time. How much television do you watch? What kind of programs? How about social media? Mindless games? Studies have shown that a typical hourly worker watches around thirty hours of television per week, while his boss watches only ten and *his* boss closer to five. Do you see the correlation? In addition, the five hours the boss is watching is most likely something educational. This person has figured out what to do with down time effectively. This is not to say we can't enjoy ourselves. We all need time to relax and enjoy family and friends. It's about what we do with the majority of our hours.

* * *

Imagine you were ten times wiser. Would that affect other aspects of your life including your job? Might that have an effect on others, co-workers, family, practically everyone you come in contact with?

I had a personal experience with this thirty years ago. I was frustrated with my workload. I had ideas for improvement but lacked the skills I needed to accomplish change, so I turned to our IT department for assistance. They said they weren't staffed to help. Essentially, the message was that I should take a class and do it myself. I was already working sixty hours per week and didn't feel that was an option.

Sharing my frustration at lunch a coworker said, "Our company could be gone tomorrow, but anything you learn while you are here could never be taken away."

Ouch! As much as that hurt, I couldn't shake those words. I realized he was right. I took the class, put in a few more hours short term and eventually was able to turn a sixty-hour workweek into forty-five. In addition, I found other applications for this new knowledge and shared it with others both at work and home. My boss took notice which led to more opportunities and advancement.

The course I took was called Lotus 1-2-3, which is today's version of Microsoft Excel. I had an immediate use for this knowledge and knew right away how I could use this new-found skill. Primarily it was for work but once I got home, I worked with it to create my own financial tracking.

Some years later I took over a position as golf league secretary for my golf league. The person who had the responsibility prior showed me how he had done the job. Basically, he used a notebook with a calculator. Right away I saw how I could computerize the process and do the work that had taken him four to five hours down to an hour or less.

As my career path progressed and I advanced in responsibility, I supervised a larger and more diverse group of people. At one point, I remember an older gentleman who didn't see the need in learning computer skills. I observed him working and noticed him doing a repetitive process of copying information down weekly. Seventy percent of the information didn't change, but his list was recreated each Monday. It only took a half an hour, but it was thirty minutes every Monday. I saw how if the data was in a spreadsheet and he only changed the data that changed weekly, he could cut the thirty minutes to ten.

I showed him how the spreadsheet was set up and how easy it was to use. I showed him the power of the calculation process and asked if he could think of any uses for himself. We put in some 401k numbers and noticed how easy it was to track gains/ losses and project where his money would move. Once he saw how it affected him personally and the ease of use, he was open to applying it to work-related tasks.

Spreadsheet knowledge was also applicable in my role at home when I taught my ten-year-old son how to use them. As golf league secretary my earnings were twenty dollars per week, which I gladly offered to my son if he would input golf statistics into a spreadsheet. I explained the details of the work to him and discussed how serious the commitment was. If there was an error, it would reflect poorly on *me* to the other members of the league. My son worked very hard his first week. Once completed, I checked his work and noted that for every mistake he would be docked five dollars. He understood.

As I reviewed his work (that had taken twice the time it took me) I found three errors. Therefore, his first weeks' pay for several hours of work was five dollars. Needless to say I never found another mistake after that. It hurt me as a dad to follow through, but I thought it was a lesson worth learning. Looking back, I'm glad I did just that.

These are examples of how I took a personal learning opportunity and applied it to other areas in my life; in this case with my co-workers, my golf league, and my family. Throughout my life, I have become known as a person who is willing to help anyone. I really take pride in teaching someone something that I have learned.

Another example of my personal development helping others in my life is a time when I learned pivot tables. The concept was an upgrade to Excel that shortened a half dozen steps to one. Once I mastered the new approach, I coached other people on how it worked. Our IT department taught a series of courses via modules. One woman outside my group mentioned that she really needed to learn new processes in Excel, but she hated to take an eight-hour class to do so. I asked her if she had a spreadsheet where she needed pivot table work. She did, so I offered to assist if she had five minutes. I showed her what I knew, and she couldn't believe how easy it was.

I attended three more Peter Lowe seminars over a period of ten years, always with a group of other associates. On my third and final trip, I was in Dayton, Ohio and Zig Ziglar was speaking. By now, I was an even bigger fan (if that's possible) and at the conclusion of his presentation he drew three names for door prizes. Out of 12,000 people, I was the third and final name chosen.

When I arrived at the booth to pick up my prize, I took a chance and asked if I could select something else. The intended prize would have been fine, but I really preferred something else. The attendant said that wasn't a problem, as Mr. Ziglar was just advertising the various products he had for sale. I was free to choose anything from the list. As my eyes scanned the order page, I saw each product listed, including, "The whole shootin match." I asked, "Does this mean I can get everything?"

The attendant said, "Sure, if that's what you want." I selected what seemed like a too-good-to-be-true prize, then started my trip back to my seat. I was carrying books, CD's, VCR cassettes, etc. All in all, I had over $1,000 dollars' worth of retail products. Since I was there on the company's time and money, I didn't feel right keeping it. Instead, I created a library offering any item to anyone to be borrowed. I wrote something in our departmental newsletter detailing the items available. The discouraging part of this was some five years later very few people had taken advantage of the free opportunity. I got in the habit of listening to CD's to and from work, Zig referred to this as "Automobile University". He was famous for adding you don't just sit there to get there. You may have resources available at your workplace as well--have you taken advantage of them? Public libraries are another excellent source of free personal development material. Not only can you borrow physical copies of books, but you can also check out audiobooks on CD, or ebooks in digital or audio format. Classes are often offered free of charge at libraries too. In the last several years, podcasts have become a widely known source for learning. Maybe you too can turn your daily commute into an Automobile University, as I was able to do when utilizing the resources, I won attending seminars. So many personal development resources are available for free.

I have heard other personal development experts--Brian Tracy, Jack Canfield, Jim Rohn--suggest similar concepts about using your commute to learn something new. Consider that if you drive 15,000 miles per year, that means you're sitting in the car over 300 hours. If you are listening to educational material rather than talk radio or music, you could obtain the equivalent of an extra year of college.

* * *

"The number one skill for the twenty-first century is the *ability* to learn new skills."
- *Peter Drucker, consultant, educator, author, and expert in modern management.*

"Every two years, you'll lose half of everything you know or else it will become irrelevant."
- *Steven Covey, author of 'The Seven Habits of Highly Effective People.'*

"If you aren't getting better, you're getting worse."
- *Pat Riley, champion basketball coach*

* * *

Warren Buffet, when discussing personal development, borrowed an idea from Benjamin Franklin. Figuring if it worked for one of the greatest men in history it would be good for him to try as well. The thought was this: Think of a person you truly admire. When you do, you'll most likely recall some things they've done or said that made you really look up to them.

Then write down everything and anything that makes you feel this way. It could be one-word phrases like honesty, integrity, faithful, or it might be phrases such as always willing to do more than expected and so on. The main point is to write everything that comes to mind. Be sure to document anything you admire.

The second part of this exercise is to think of someone you'd rather not be around, or dislike. Again, start writing every reason that comes to mind on what you see as negative.

Now once you've compiled those lists review the positive qualities and words you wrote about the person you admire. Make a commitment to yourself that you will live your life trying to attain every word or phrase documented. Likewise, review the negative aspects and again commit to live a life that never would cause someone to criticize you with those types of words.

Buffett said, "If it worked for Franklin, it would certainly be worth trying to copy for himself."

What I Know: I'm only going to be a better person if I'm intentional with my time and actions. This includes reading regularly and being around great people. People who aren't negative and inspire me to be my best.

What I've Learned: To take advantage of opportunities to learn. #1 Automobile University. While I was working I got in the habit of listening to motivational audiobooks on my commute daily. This totaled more than an hour per day of learning that would have otherwise been wasted on mindless talk radio or music. Those hours of learning assisted greatly in my outlook on life and what I was able to share with others.

What I've Read: Where do I start? I am always reading something on a topic that will teach me something new. A list of my top fifty personal development books is listed at the end of this chapter.

What Makes Sense: I am only going to improve by reading, gaining new insights, new ideas, and by listening to great people. Speaking only reinforces what I know, therefore, to learn I must be a good listener.

Best Story: When I was young, I wanted to change the world, when I saw I couldn't change the world I tried to change my country. When I saw I couldn't change my country, I tried to change my town. When I saw I couldn't change my town, I tried to change my family. When I saw I couldn't, I realized if I'd changed myself, I'd have influenced my family, they would have influenced our town, and our town would have influenced our country, and our country would have influenced the world.

Best Lesson: Why we need personal development: helping yourself in order to help others. Apply your own oxygen mask before securing someone else's. If I'm not around, I can do no earthly good to anyone.

Best Quote: A person who won't read has no advantage over the person who can't read. Ignorance is expensive.

Where to go for More:
https://www.success.com/category/personal-development/: This is the personal development blog portion of success.com, which is a small section of a huge resource of success driven resources.
https://www.jimrohn.com/category/blog/personal-development/: Jim Rohn, notably one of the leading experts in personal and business development, offers several resources on the topic of personal development.

http://www.jongordon.com/ : Jon Gordon provides free downloads and weekly newsletters with featured stories. He also has a weekly podcast I never miss

http:/www.benjaminhardy.com : Benjamin Hardy has a free 30 day course I'd highly recommend. He is a blogger and has many videos on YouTube for free

http://www.awarebc.com/ : Featuring old clips of Zig Ziglar, this podcast highlights some of the best pieces of advice around personal development.

http://www.ignite80.com/: Ron Friedman touches on different aspects of personal development through monthly tips.

http://www.harveymackay.com/: This site provides a weekly newsletter on personal development.

The Eight Facets of Life Facebook Page: Shameless plug, and also a page where I will share various resources and current articles on the topics related to this book.

* * *

Basic mistakes people make:

1) not reading quality material
2) not realizing the impact of not reading
3) not utilizing their time wisely
4) filling their mind with negativity
5) looking at the cost of a book or a seminar instead of the value received

* * *

Questions to consider: On a scale of 1 – 10 with 10 being perfection how would you rate yourself in this area:

The 8 Facets of Life

1) How many books have I read in the past year? _____

2) Do you currently use Automobile University? Y N hours per week _____

3) Are my friends / coworkers' acquaintances highly motivated? Y N

4) How many hours of TV / social media / video games etc. per day? _____

5) How many e-zines, newsletters, etc. are you subscribed to and read? _____

6) How many podcasts or webinars do you listen to per week? _____

7) When I read am I in the habit of underlining or taking notes? _____

Take Away:

- Make personal development an important part of the rest of your life. Get a library card, subscribe to e-zines and newsletters. Browse the free podcasts available on your device. Take good notes, attend seminars, lectures, and church. Sit in the front row, expect to learn. Buy or borrow audiobooks etc. When you read a book that you own, have a highlighter in hand. Mark the key points or interesting facts. Don't let the cost deter you. Utilize used book stores or garage sales for great deals on personal development resources.

- Highlighting a sentence or phrase may help retain the information. It may also help you find those key points faster at a later date. Many times, I'll pick up a book I've read and scan just the highlights. This might take twenty minutes versus rereading the book.

- Turn your car into Automobile University. Don't just sit there to get there, listen to an audiobook or podcast.
- Invest in yourself, increase your self-esteem, self-respect, and your personal pride. Plus, when you take the time to read something, you may find the material motivates me beyond where you were when you started. It's similar to the feeling I get after a physical workout at the gym. I've invested in my physical health whereas with reading I'm investing in my mental health and beyond.

Best Tip: Work harder on yourself than you do on your job.

Imagine being born into the world as a one-pound block of steel. Another person is born as a one-pound block of gold. Your worth might be $10 while the gold is around $20,000.

But if we machine the one-pound block of steel into watch springs the value can exceed $25,000. You get the point, it's not what you come into the world with, but what we make of ourselves while we're here, and the difference we make in others. That's personal development.

Bonus: Below is a list of books I've read that I can personally recommend. I'd classify them all personal development books but remember what I mentioned at the beginning of the chapter, personal development can and most likely will cross over to the other aspects of our life as well.

The Bible--If you've never read this, I'd recommend not starting in Genesis and reading through Revelation. I'd recommend instead starting with a gospel like John and reading it. Then you could read the other gospels, Matthew, Mark, and Luke and see the similarities as well as differences. Another of my favorites is Proverbs. I've heard of businessmen who read Proverbs every month. One chapter per day. Another way to read *The Bible* is to look at the concordance in the back for a subject you'd like to learn more about. As an example, look up wisdom and you'll get a variety of passages to review to gain knowledge. The same applies to money, depression, etc.

Twelve Pillars, by Jim Rohn and Chris Widener--This book is all about personal development. It's a rare fiction book I've read that tells a great story of how to acquire wisdom.

The One Minute Manager by Ken Blanchard and Spencer Johnson--This is a quick read, another fiction book that is written as a tale of business and career enhancement with the same principles applied to managing a home, etc.

The Traveler's Gift: Seven Decisions that Determine Personal Success by Andy Andrews---Another fiction title that tells a great story and really makes you think.

The Butterfly Effect: How Your Life Matters by Andy Andrews--A great book to give to someone as a gift that shows how the smallest of actions on our part can have a ripple effect.

Leadership and Self Deception: Getting Out of the Box by The Arbinger Institute--A great book on how we view people. Eye opening.

The Outward Mindset: Seeing Beyond Ourselves by The Arbinger Institute--A follow up to *Leadership and Self Deception* with some real-life examples.

It's Your Call: What Are You Doing Here? by Gary Barkalow--The book is about figuring out your calling or purpose in life.

The Success Principles: How to Get from Where You Are To Where You Want to Be by Jack Canfield--Canfield details several principles he's uncovered and explained with tips.

High Performance Habits: How Extraordinary People Become That Way by Brendon Burchard

PERSONAL DEVELOPMENT

The Magic of Thinking Big by David Schwartz and Jason Culp

The Seven Habits of Highly Effective People: Powerful Lessons in Personal Change by Steven Covey--I highlighted many, many pages in this book.

See You at The Top by Zig Ziglar

Over the Top: Moving From Survival to Stability, From Stability to Success, From Success to Significance by Zig Ziglar

The Five Love Languages: The Secret to Love That Lasts by Gary Chapman--This book will be recommended again in the chapter on marriage, must read.

Think Big: Unleashing Your Potential for Excellence by Ben Carson

Good to Great: Why Some Companies Make the Leap... And Others Don't by Jim Collins

Uncommon: Finding Your Path to Significance by Tony Dungy

Mindset by Carol Dweck--This is another must read book. I recommend it again in the section on family.

The Four Doors: A Guide to Freedom, Joy, and a Meaningful Life by Richard Paul Evans

The Energy Bus: 10 Rules to Fuel Your Life, Work, and Team with Positive Energy by Jon Gordon--This book is a fictional tale with a major lesson.

The Seed: Finding Purpose and Happiness in Life and Work by Jon Gordon

Training Camp: What the Best Do Better Than Everyone Else by Jon Gordon

Talk Like Ted: The 9 Public Speaking Secrets of the World's To Minds by Carmine Gallo

Blink: The Power of Thinking Without Thinking, *The Tipping Point: How Little Things Can Make a Big Difference*, and *Outliers: The Story of Success* by Malcom Gladwell--These books share a lot of how we do things and why.

The Compound Effect: Multiply Your Success One Simple Step at a Time by Darren Hardy--This book discusses how small, seemingly insignificant choices, add up to big results.

Living Forward: A Proven Plan to Stop Drifting and Get the Life You Want by Michael Hyatt and Daniel Harkavy

Your Best Year Ever: A 5-Step Plan for Achieving Your Most Important Goals by Michael Hyatt

Switch: How to Change Things When Change Is Hard and *Made to Stick: Why Some Ideas Survive and Others Die* by Chip and Dan Heath

Outlive Your Life: You Were Made to Make a Difference by Max Lucado

Dream Job: 48 Days to the Work You Love by Dan Miller

A Million Miles in a Thousand Years: What I Learned While Editing My Life by Donald Miller

What God Wants Every Dad to Know: The Most Important Principles to Teach Your Child by James Merritt

All Pro Dad: Seven Essentials to Be a Hero to Your Child by Mark Merrill

The Fred Factor: How Passion in Your Work and Life Can Turn the Ordinary Into the Extraordinary by Mark Sanborn

The Last Lecture by Randy Pausch--Pausch tells the story of a man who is dying and wanting to leave a message for his young children.

Personal Development

The Slight Edge: Turning Simple Disciplines into Massive Success and Happiness by Jeff Olson

Become a Better You: 7 Keys to Improving Your Life Every Day and *Your Best Life Now: 7 Steps to Living at Your Full Potential* by Joel Osteen

Procrastinate on Purpose: 5 Permissions to Multiply Your Time and *Take the Stairs: 7 Steps to Achieving True Success* by Rory Vaden

Wooden: A Lifetime of Observations and Reflections on and off the Court by John Wooden, Steve Jamison, et al.

The Happiness Advantage: The Seven Principles of Positive Psychology That Fuel Success and Performance at Work and *Before Happiness: The Five Hidden Keys to Achieving Success, Spreading Happiness, and Sustaining Positive Change* by Shawn Achor

Today Matters: 12 Daily Practices to Guarantee Tomorrow's Success and *Everyone Communicates, Few Connect: What the Most Effective People Do Differently* by John C. Maxwell

The Purpose Driven Life: What on Earth Am I Here For? by Rick Warren

Start with Why: How Great Leaders Inspire Everyone to Take Action by Simon Sinek

Lead for God's Sake!: A Parable for Finding the Heart of Leadership by Todd Gongwer

CHAPTER 2

FAMILY

*A truly rich man is one whose children run
into his arms when his hands are empty.*

What is it? Some might argue with today's definition of family. For this writing however I'd like to consider my family to be those we hold closest. For me that's my wife and two sons, along with their families.

When I've taught *The Eight Facets* to groups and I've asked them to rank the eight in terms of importance, family has always been first or second. What I've found, however, is despite what we say, oftentimes our hours are spent elsewhere. Additionally, for the goal setters among us, I've never heard of anyone setting a *family goal*. I'll admit to that; I never even considered it until the last twenty years of my life. I had set goals for career, health, and finance and figured I had the bases covered. One day I realized with that type of thinking, family and everything else would simply get what's left.

I admit to primarily leaving the process to OJT (on the job training). I think most of us, if we're honest, would admit the same. We see how others interact with their families, learning from the good and the bad. Hopefully we can then expand on what is good and eliminate what we perceive as bad.

Around the age of thirty, I got hooked on learning about personal development. I started reading and listening to books and attending presentations surrounding the topic. It's not to say I think the so-called experts have it all figured out, but I realized if I was open to what worked for others, I could then apply it myself, if it made sense. What I'll share is either what worked for me or what I've learned from others.

I believe family is two distinct pieces: marriage and children. I'll start with marriage because I believe it's the most important piece to the family puzzle. If the husband – wife relationship is on solid ground the family unit can operate like a well-oiled machine. If not, bringing children along before it is stable could be a recipe for disaster. Therefore, let's start with marriage.

Marriage

My wife and I were married at twenty-one after dating for three years. I would say our dating was what I saw others do at that time: movies, dining out, and softball games. We probably saw each other four to five times per week. I held two jobs saving for a house.

My expectations were that marriage would be just like dating, only I wouldn't have to take her home at midnight. I'm not sure what my wife's expectations were because we never discussed it. We did do some pre-marital counseling with our preacher, but there were some demographic barriers and I'm not truly certain that we took away all that we could have. I think we were more mature than most our age, but I can see now that we could have been better prepared.

What if?

My oldest son told me that prior to his marriage he went through some marriage counseling that was several sessions and ended with a daylong event with other soon-to-be wed couples. He mentioned they were given several real-life scenarios and asked to talk through them. One example: Where will you gather for holidays? He said it was a real eye opener because both had assumed they'd be at *their* parent's homes for holidays. Talking through an issue like those months prior to it ever happening allowed some civil discussion. In addition, it led to more talks about other issues they could see arising.

The more things that can be discussed prior to them actually happening the better. Even if you don't go through formal counseling you can come up with your own set of questions or life what-if's.

Here are some ideas to consider before getting married or to discuss if you are already married:

1. YOUR SPOUSE IS NOT GOING TO COMPLETE YOU.

   "It's important for you to focus on you — not in a selfish way, not in a way that disregards your partner, but in a way where you understand taking care of yourself is going to help you bring your best self to your relationship.

2. BE AWARE OF THE EXPECTATIONS YOU'RE BRINGING INTO THE MARRIAGE.

   You probably want <u>a lot from just one person</u>: A companion, a passionate lover, good parent and more. Here are some expectations couples may expect:

   My partner will meet all of my needs for companionship.

   I don't believe romance should fade over time.

   - I don't believe that my partner's <u>interest in sex</u> should be different than mine.

- We will visit my parents weekly but his monthly because of the distance to travel

3. YOU WON'T ALWAYS FEEL "IN LOVE."

    "You could be with the most perfect partner in the world for you and you're going to go through seasons where you feel like you're not aligned and you're not in love,". "That's where it's really important to be grounded in the values that you identify as a couple, versus trying to follow the feelings that you think you're supposed to be having."

4. YOUR PARTNER'S FAMILY RELATIONSHIPS ARE KEY.

    How did your partner get along with his family? Were they close or distant? Was there conflict? That information is important to understand.

    "Many of the themes in our family repeat or resurface in marriage. When couples are able to talk about that stuff without judgment, are able to listen and tune into their partner's experience, it's huge. It creates a deep level of trust."

5. KNOW YOUR PARTNER'S FINANCES.

    You should both disclose your entire financial situations. From there, start to decide: What's the best way to <u>manage the finances</u>? Many young couples today have one joint account, plus their own separate accounts.

    "That's fine, if that's what works. But you want to talk about it to make sure that's not because you are feeling controlled or you're bringing in insecurities. Finances are where the mistrust and issues can surface. It's one of the top reasons people divorce. For that reason my wife and I had only joint accounts.

Money can be such a touchy topic that for some couples, talking about it can be more uncomfortable than discussing sex.

6. CONFLICT IS INEVITABLE — RECOGNIZE YOUR ROLE IN RESOLVING IT.

When you're in the honeymoon phase, it's hard to imagine there will be arguments or that your spouse has annoying traits and habits, but all of that awaits. How will you deal?

Often, the things you dislike or despise later in your relationship <u>have more to do with</u> *you* than your partner.

"A big piece about how to handle conflict and anger is knowing that it starts with yourself... how you can manage your own thoughts and practice healthy ways of taking care of you.

From there, it's about knowing how to come together and communicate as a couple. People are very quick to respond and react, but what you need to do is stop, be present and listen.

7. DISCUSS WHAT A BREACH OF TRUST WOULD MEAN TO YOU.

What would a <u>betrayal</u> mean to you? For some people, unacceptable behavior can mean flirting, sending texts or having an emotional affair. For others, the only deal-breaker may be sleeping with someone else. Talk about it before you get married.

8. WHEN THE GOING GETS TOUGH, DON'T CALL IT QUITS RIGHT AWAY.

Many young married couples <u>get divorced</u> very soon — less than five years into their marriage.

"There's a mentality in our world today that if something's not working for you, get rid of it.

"But conflicts in marriages and relationships are opportunities to grow."

Unless you're experiencing abuse or other intolerable behavior, give yourself the chance to try to work things out.

I've known many people who after getting a divorce said, looking back it was the worst thing they could have done. Realize what you've got, it's hard to unsaw sawdust.

9. 9. EXPRESS LOVE

Research by psychologist John Gottman found a "magic" 5-to-1 ratio among healthy couples: For every one negative interaction during a conflict, people in a stable and happy marriage had five or more positive interactions.

The positivity is crucial. It's really important to feel like you're in a good place, and that is definitely shown through the little acts of love. Not the big things, like planning lavish trips or spending a million bucks on your partner, but just waking up in the morning and giving them a kiss.

How Does a Good Marriage Work?

Most of my ideas of how a good marriage worked came from watching my parents. I don't ever recall them arguing in front of us kids. Mom ran the household, and Dad was the provider. They shared parenting in terms of discipline, although Dad was the one who put fear in us (most likely the same for anyone growing up in the sixties).

My image of a good husband came from those observances as well as my own experiences in dating. I have heard it said that a man enters marriage hoping his wife won't change, and a wife enters marriage hoping to change her husband. That seems comical in a way but also true, at least from my viewpoint.

I have since learned more about being a good husband from church, be it sermons or Bible readings and devotions. One preacher I like to listen to is Atlanta-based James Merritt. He has a series on marriage explaining that we enter into a marriage with different expectations. We often have the mindset that *this is what I want*, not *what I want to give*. He further adds that having a happy marriage that ends happily ever after is not in finding the right person, but in *being* the right person. Even though that thought process goes against our normal way of thinking I buy into what he's saying 100%.

Many people say that they found Mister or Miss Right, but what I really think they are saying is they were compatible. I've seen couples who could finish each other's sentences. Does that mean their marriage is any happier than any other? I don't think so.

So, what does it mean to be the right kind of person? This could probably be an entire chapter in a marriage book but I'll throw out a few things that are important to me. First, to be the right person to my wife, I'm always 100% honest, I'll never cheat or look elsewhere to have my needs met. I'll say when I'm sad and when I'm happy. She does not have to guess.

This leads me to **feedback**. I first heard Jack Canfield, author of the popular *Chicken Soup for the Soul* series, suggest giving feedback, something he does regularly in his own marriage. To do this, he suggests asking your spouse on a scale of one to ten, *how would you rate our marriage* every week. Anything less than a ten gets a follow-up question, *what would it take to make it a ten?* Canfield further asks, in general, if we don't offer feedback, will my wife tell her friends, her mom, maybe even her hairdresser what's wrong?

If so, the one person who can do anything about the problem is left out in the cold.

Giving and receiving feedback about the state of your marriage can be so beneficial. If you have an issue, tell your spouse. Talk to each other about the state of your marriage weekly, and follow up when issues arise. Be clear on your feedback, both husband and wife. Also, be sure each gets the opportunity to share. Remember it's not one sided. Both of you are trying to be the right person for each other in your marriage.

The following are traits of a strong marriage. How many would you apply to your relationship? Which of the following are areas that need attention?

1. **You have a strong trust in each other.** At the heart of a good marriage is trust. If you know that your spouse has a deep trust in you and you feel the same about them, that goes a long way.
2. **You enjoy spending time together.** There's nobody I'd rather go to dinner with than my wife. I'm the happiest when we are together. She understands me. And when I'm with her, I feel like we're a team.
3. **You put the other first.** With kids, work, activities, and everything else in life, it's hard to make your spouse a priority. But when you're with the right person, you make sure you prioritize that relationship. Showing you appreciate that person -- and doing little things, things you did in the beginning of the relationship -- indicates you're a good match.
4. **Your spouse doesn't always have to be right.** You want a person who's willing to invest energy into developing and maintaining a strong marriage relationship, says Mark E. Sharp, a psychologist that specializes in relationship issues. That means the person is open to

hearing your viewpoints and considering alternative experiences, not someone who insists that his viewpoint is the only viewpoint.

5. **You have mutual respect.** While some people think shared interests is a strong indicator, Joanna Dyanes, mom to three kids in Chicago, Illinois, thinks it's really respect that matters. "My husband loves sports. I hate them. I love to go out and socialize, he's a homebody. And yet I know without a doubt that he's the right person for me. I respect him enough to give him his sports and alone time because I know it's important to him. He loves and respects me enough that it doesn't bother him that I'm at book club or cooking club or PTA many weeknights. We respect who the other person is and that means giving them time to enjoy their interests."

6. **You make each other laugh.** Life can be really hard at times, and you need someone by your side who can lighten your mood. A well-placed comment or story shared at the right time can be just what the doctor ordered.

7. **You treat each other with kindness.** Being in a good marriage means remembering to be nice to each other and to apologize sincerely when you're wrong, says Lottie Grimes, a licensed professional counselor. Saying "I'm sorry" is never easy, but those couples in a good marriage know it's important to say those words – and mean it.

8. **You're excited about the future together.** Whether it's taking a family trip, attending your child's kindergarten graduation, or planning a date night, if you're excited about planning the future with your partner, that's a sign you married the right one.

From a young age I heard that in order to be happily married, you need only to find the right person. Having lived many years, I have come to the conclusion that this idea is entirely false. I believe that marriage is not about finding the right person, but rather about becoming the right person. When you focus on your own behaviors and the way you treat the person you love, it will not be long before things begin to change. None of us have the power or ability to change another human being. We cannot make someone do what we want them to do. But we can make ourselves do what we need to do in order to become the kind of person who is worthy of being in a good, healthy relationship. Perhaps a humorous story will help.

Did you hear about the man who was sick of his wife and wanted a divorce? He went to see an attorney in order to get some advice. The attorney asked the man if he really wanted to hurt his wife badly in the divorce. The man replied, "Absolutely!" The attorney said, "Then here is what you should do. For the next thirty days I want you to go out of your way to be nice to her. Send her flowers, call her every day, take her to her favorite restaurants, take her to movies that she likes, and go shopping with her. Do everything in your power to show her how much you love and care about her and want to meet her needs. Then, after thirty days, when she is madly in love with you, that is when we will file the divorce action. It will totally catch her off guard and will hurt her deeply."

Well, when the man heard this, he was delighted. He thought that was great advice. So, without any hesitation, he went into action. For the next thirty days he poured his time, effort, attention, money, resources, and everything else into his relationship with his wife. They went to movies, plays, concerts, out to eat, took trips together - it was incredible! He showered her with kindness, love, gentleness, and words of encouragement daily. At the end of thirty days, the attorney called and asked if he was ready to file the divorce action against his wife. The man replied, "Are you kidding? Why would I want to divorce this woman? She is the woman of my dreams! I am so in love with her I can hardly wait to see her every day. Why would I ever want to divorce someone as wonderful as this?!"

Although that is a humorous story, it does press the point I am trying to make. You see, when the man changed the way he was behaving towards his wife, everything changed. He no longer focused on what she was doing wrong; rather, he focused on what he could do right. In other words, when he became the right kind of person, the situation began to change. He also learned the truth found in the principle, "Where your treasure is - there will your heart be also." I honestly believe that is the key to a happy marriage and a happy relationship. It is not trying to control another person or force them to do what you want them to do; it is simply making yourself do what you should do in order to demonstrate love to the other person.

I once heard a definition of love and I certainly agree with it: Love is giving of yourself to another person in order to meet their basic needs without having any expectations in return. When you give of your time, effort and attention to another person in order to meet their basic needs, then real love will begin to happen. The key is in understanding their personality style and understanding the things that make them happy, expecting nothing in return. It is the same principle of "give and it will be given unto you." Notice you must give first before anything comes in return. And sometimes that takes time.

Love is perhaps one of the most misinterpreted concepts in our culture. If you watch television and movies, love is always equated with a physical relationship. Yet, I believe much more is included in a romantic relationship than just the physical aspect. I have seen a mate sit by the side of a loved one in the hospital, holding their hand, rubbing their back, or putting a cold washcloth on their face in order to help them feel better. Although that is not everything that love is about, I certainly think it is a good picture of real, true love because they are meeting another person's basic needs and not expecting them to do anything for them in return. That is genuine love at its best!

If you get one concept or idea from this that will help you be a good person, more worthy of being in a healthy relationship, then this will have done its job. Focus on what you can do to make things better without any hidden agenda toward the other person and watch what happens!

Marriage tips from Family Circle post by googling Marriage Tips.

1. **Have a "growth mind-set."**

    Be a lifelong learner. If both of you are willing to learn from your mistakes and the challenges in your relationship, you will thrive as individuals and as a couple.

2. **Take good care of yourself.**

    You can't give from an empty cup. Keep up your self-care no matter what. This is especially important for women, who often give until depleted and then nobody's happy.

3. **Let go of perfectionism—your partner isn't perfect, and neither are you.**

    In all relationships, both partners will make mistakes. Don't let perfectionism destroy what is overall a good, solid, loving relationship. Be kind to yourself and be kind to your sweetheart.

4. **Say "appreciations" often before going to sleep.**

    Right before drifting off to sleep, share a few things that you appreciate about each other. (Three is a good number, but feel free to share more.) It could be something you did that day or a quality (like "I love how honest you are with me") you value. Focus on what you love and appreciate about each other and you will find more to love and appreciate.

5. **Remember: Men want respect, and women want to be cherished.**

    Women: Be respectful and kind to your man and he will cherish you. Men: Cherish and be kind to your woman and she will respect you. Win-win!

6. **Practice forgiveness—not just forgiving your spouse, but forgiving yourself.**

    We interviewed couples that had been happily married for more than 50 years. One of their secrets? Being willing to forgive. Practice forgiveness for your partner's mistakes and for your own. (See number 3, above.)

7. **Never threaten divorce. That's the kiss of death.**

    Don't throw around the threat of divorce, even in the heat of an argument. Your marriage is too important and too sacred to threaten to end it over an argument.

8. **Practice "the simmer" (and don't forget to "deliver").**

    You want to keep your relationship on simmer and then gradually and consistently bring it to a boil. What does that mean? It means flirt with your partner. Send each other sexy texts. Pat him on the butt when you pass him in the kitchen. Give her a long lingering kiss over the laundry. And then remember to let that simmer turn into a full-blown boil regularly. Enjoy yourself. Regular sex is important in your relationship for so many reasons.

9. **Allow yourself to be vulnerable with each other.**

    Brené Brown said, "What makes you vulnerable makes you beautiful." Opening your heart and sharing your tender places with your spouse creates real intimacy and connection. Always be willing to share your true, deep, scary feelings. This helps create a bond that will last. And ladies, please know that his vulnerability may look different than yours. That's okay.

10. **Marry the right person.**

    After over 10 years of coaching women to do the inner work to prepare to find love, we've seen over and over again that the personal growth investments of time, energy and resources BEFORE you meet your future spouse have a return that is exponential. You have a higher chance of attracting a quality person who will stick by you when you have learned how your beliefs and behaviors create your circumstances. Your past does not have to equal your future!

A preacher once said that most people look for a person who can satisfy all their needs. Once they find them, they realize they only fill 80%, so they may look to have the 20% lacking fulfilled by someone else. Only to realize no one has the whole package. If they find the 20% that was lacking in another, chances are they'll be lacking in an area they took for granted from their first marriage. Be grateful for the 80% you have rather than the 20% that's lacking.

Zig Ziglar had some information he shared once that said the data suggests 50% of all marriages fail. This was wrong because the data was simply the number of divorce filings compared to the number of marriage licenses issued over a period of time. His data indicated the number of successful marriages was closer to 80% because many people that had a failed marriage, many times had multiple failed marriages. This skewed the data.

Marriage is a commitment, not a feeling. Truth is, no two people are completely compatible. We have to learn to become one. That means we may have to make sacrifices; we may have to overlook some things. We must be willing to compromise for the good of the relationship.

I recall a story I once heard. A woman explained how she had nagged her husband constantly to put his clothes away, help out more, and several other things. Finally, she complimented him on one thing he did right, despite the several he still did wrong. As time progressed, he did more and more things right and even did some repairs around the house that he'd been putting off. By focusing on the good, she got more, whereas when we focus on the bad, we'll usually reap more of the same. This makes all the sense in the world but it usually isn't what we think of to do.

Another story in the book, A Million Miles in a Thousand Years, Donald Miller tells of a woman answering questions from a live audience and a question came up asking, did she believe there was only one true love for every person? She essentially said no, and she said that with her husband sitting right there in the audience. She added that she and her husband believed they were a cherished prize for each other, and they most likely would drive other people mad. But she added, she married a guy, and he was just a guy. He wasn't going to make all her problems go away, because he was just a guy. And that freed her to love him as a guy, not as an ultimate problem solver. And because her husband believed she was just a girl; he was free to love her as well. Neither needed the other to make everything ok. They were simply content to have good company through life's conflicts and joyous events as well.

I'd like to share one last story that illustrates for me how to make a strong marriage. The speaker shared the image of two rowboats. Husband in one, wife in the other. If both just let the wind take them where it may, soon they'll wind up far apart and wonder how it happened. However, if together they are rowing and working to stay together, they'll arrive at their destination. It takes some work, by both parties. Sometimes, lots of work. But it's worth it, as most would testify. I think a key problem of today's marriages is that oftentimes a spouse will say, if not verbally at least by their actions, my children are number one in my life. I think it's great to feel a closeness to our children and want what's best for them. However, the truth is they will be with us for a very short time in our lives as compared to our spouse. In my opinion our spouse is the most important human being on this earth and it's important that our children understand that.

If we as spouses don't show love to each other, our children will see that and feel it and there is a good chance they will mimic our actions in their own marriages later.

The best book I ever read on marriage that opened my eyes was *The Five Love Languages* by Gary Chapman. Actually, this was the first book I ever listened to as an audiobook. Several people had recommended it to me but I kept shrugging it off. The title didn't speak to me. Finally, I gave in and am sure glad I did. It was eye opening. In the book, Chapman explains that we all have a primary and a secondary love language. The love languages are words of affirmation, physical touch, gifts, acts of service, and quality time.

Chapman goes on to say that since we all have a primary love language and the fact that opposites attract the chances are my spouse and I don't have the same love language. As an example, if my primary love language is words of affirmation, what that's saying is I long to hear her tell me that she loves me and why. If she is constantly complaining about what's not done around the house my love tank is most likely running on empty.

On the other hand, if my wife's primary love language is acts of service but I never help out around the house, then she's not feeling loved. I could shower her with gifts as well as tell her I love her, but those feelings of love won't take the place. Once hearing this and giving it some thought it made so much sense to me. I had to go out and buy the book and have since given several copies to others. I'd highly recommend reading and figuring out yours and your partner's love languages. You can even do a free assessment on his website https://www.5lovelanguages.com/quizzes/.

A great book I read about treating people as people and not objects is *Leadership and Self Deception* from the Arbinger Institute. In it is an example about a husband and wife with a newborn child. Imagine the baby starts crying in the middle of the night. You hear it (husband) but you've worked all day and know you need your sleep. You figure your wife will certainly get up and take care of the baby.

Time goes by and no movement by her. You start thinking to yourself, surely, she hears this, she is just faking being asleep, she's a bad mom, she is lazy, a lousy wife, inconsiderate. The longer you lay there you start to see yourself as the victim, you're a good dad, a good husband. Do these thoughts and feelings help you to reconsider your decision on what you should do? No! They justify why you're not.

This goes much deeper than I can explain in a couple paragraphs, but generally if we do what needs done--rather than expecting our spouse to take care of it-- life goes on and we are a team. When we don't do tasks for each other we deceive ourselves. The longer the task is left undone, the more we justify our lack of support as the other is not deserving.

Another recent book I read mentioned that couples need a ratio of five to one in favor of positive feedback to have a thriving marriage. Couples who tend to needle each other even if over trivial issues have a divorce rate much higher than those who have an occasional blowup but keep to the aforementioned ratio.

Here's a tip that is easier said than done and I'll mention it again in raising children. You have to be able to transition in your role(s) from work to husband/wife. Despite what happened today, when work is over before entering the house, take a breath and tell yourself, *I'm now a husband or wife and I'm committed to being the best I can.*

If asked when is the most important time for couples, most would say first thing in the morning or right before going to bed. Although both of these are important, experts agree it's when we reconnect after being apart for work. If you think about it, these few moments set the tone for the rest of the evening. If I'm upset about how my day went or how someone treated me and it spills over into my reconnection greeting, chances are this isn't going to be a great evening.

Likewise, if my day has been good but I'm greeted by, "It's about time you are home. You won't believe the kind of day I've had! These kids are driving me crazy!" Chances are the night will not be pleasant.

So, make it a point to be pleasant upon reconnection. You can share your problems or issues at a better time but set the tone by making your spouse feel appreciated. After all you are a team, you want what's best for each other and making this a practice will set you up for marriage success.

A few facts on marriage. Married couples live longer, they are less likely to suffer serious illness and when they do, they recover quicker. The American Medical Association reported the health benefit of being married is equivalent to being ten years younger. Studies show a significantly higher level of happiness as well as mental health. Another study done involving 17 nations found that married couples were 3.4 times more likely to be happy and content with life compared to cohabiting couples.

It's been said that 90% of our disagreements could be solved if we as a couple could do one thing: show empathy. Empathy is basically looking at the situation from the other's perspective. Many people get this wrong thinking that it means giving in. That's not it. You don't necessarily give in although you could. It just means you understand why it means so much to them and they do likewise.

As an example, your wife has a doctor's appointment and wants you to accompany her. You have an important business meeting that can't be changed. Empathy doesn't mean you go. It means the two of you have a discussion and explain why. The discussion could go something like this:

Wife: I'd like you to be with me. I'm scared of what I might hear. I'm not sure how I would deal with bad news?

Husband: I understand but I can't on that day. I've been working long hours on this project and my clients are coming in from out of town. Too many people are counting on me. You know I'd be there if I could.

This is empathy. You may not like the outcome, but it shows an understanding and caring conversation between the couple. The husband has acknowledged and shown compassion towards his wife.

Another way to think about empathy is that it's like two wings of an airplane. One wing is the head or the analytical part, the other is the heart or the sympathetic piece. Typically, men are great at problem solving and women are superior with sympathetic feelings. When you can put both pieces together you have empathy.

When I first heard this metaphor, I was probably fifty years old. I'd been married for close to thirty years. The book I was listening to was explaining that men are hardwired to problem solve and women just want someone to listen, that they want to be heard. My wife was a board member for an organization and upon coming home one evening, she vented about how a part of the meeting had gone. I quickly detailed how I would handle the situation. After hearing this advice, I asked her what action she'd taken. Her reply was that she'd done nothing. I then told her about the book was listening to, asking if she wanted a solution or just wanted to be heard. She agreed with the book. She didn't want me to solve her problem, she was just bouncing her reactions to the meeting off me.

It amazes me that we could have been married that long and never known that about each other. This just further proves how different we are as men and women. I never considered she just wanted to be heard, likewise she never considered explaining. We both just thought it was common knowledge yet nothing could be further from the truth. It's not to say one is better than the other, it's just that we are different.

One of the myths of marriage is it's a 50-50 proposition. The truth is we aren't fractions. It doesn't feel fair. We have to be willing to give 100% and in return we'll receive 100%.

A tip I've heard is to ask your spouse, on a scale of 1-10 where are you internally? What are your distractions, anxiety, finance, work project etc? They may answer I'm a 3 right now because of _____ until the end of the month. This doesn't fix anything, but it helps the other spouse understand and feel empathy more easily.

Intimacy isn't a 10 every day. The question could be asked, how's your love life? This would include your commitment (your energy or focus), passion (physical), and intimacy (emotional).

Conflicts are bound to arise. The key is not to avoid conflict but how to behave fairly and how to resolve. Again, one method is to ask, on a scale of one to ten, how big of a deal is this to you? One being no big deal and ten being over my dead body. Many times, you'll find when you look at a situation like this you realize it's not worth the anger.

Another tip is how the words are used. Imagine you are driving down the road and the passenger turns the radio station. You could say, "Who made you king or queen of the radio, or why do you always have to be in control?" You could imagine what kind of reply you'd get and how the rest of the ride might go. Or you could state something that doesn't get your spouse so defensive, such as, "When I'm driving and you turn the radio station without asking, I feel ignored." This doesn't come across nearly as a critical comment.

Another point of conflict is to understand when not to talk. When one person isn't ready to talk because they need to get some facts, or to think, it's important to respect that. However, that person needs to let the other know when they'll be ready. I need thirty minutes or right after I take care of this. That may go against some wisdom but the point being once words are spoken, they can't be taken back.

Time is the second biggest complaint of married couples. The first being communication. Regarding time we know we can't make more of it. The only thing we *can* do is use what we have wisely. One way to do this is to discuss in advance the upcoming week's schedule. What's going on, when, for how long etc. If there's an issue, it's better to talk about it before it comes up. It's not to say other things might come up, or you may forget but without upfront communication everything could be a surprise.

Communication is a key to a successful marriage. Probably the most important key. One problem I see however is men and women communicate much differently and each considers their way the best. At least it's the best for them to understand. In a recent Focus on the Family publication, I found an article I'd like to share with their permission. It was titled "Creating Emotional Word Pictures" and was written by John Trent with Kari Trent Stageberg.

> "We don't talk anymore!" shouted my wife, Cindy.
> "That's ridiculous," I said. "We talk all the time!"
> "But not what we need to talk about. What's important to me? What's important for us!"
> "Then drive with me to my softball game. If it's that big of a deal, you can talk to me on the way to the game about anything you want."
>
> But Cindy wouldn't go to that game. Soon after, she wouldn't go to any of my games. I was convinced she was just emotional or intentionally not explaining what she meant. She seemed convinced that I simply didn't care about her or anything else she had to say.
>
> That was the level of communication in our first year of marriage. We talked about how we needed to communicate with each other – all the time. But we never connected. Cindy became more and more hurt and lonely and I grew more and more angry and lonely.
>
> And then the day came when things blew up – but in an amazing way. On that day, Cindy used a powerful communication tool, a word picture, to change my life… and our marriage.
>
> The story that made the difference.
>
> One morning after another night of frustration with each other, I walked into the kitchen and noticed a book on my breakfast plate. It was my thick Advanced Psychopathology textbook.
>
> "So, what's this?" I picked up the book off my plate. "This is breakfast?" I said, barely concealing my contempt.
> "No," Cindy said. "That's me."
> "I don't get it."
> "You know how last semester you were taking this class?" she asked. "You were reading this book and taking

notes on it almost every night? You really dug into it, trying to learn all that was there. Not just for a test, but because it might help you help someone someday."

I nodded tentatively.

"And what's happened to that book now that you've passed the course, now that you're on to another semester?" She didn't have to say anything. I was using it as a doorstop in my study.

Cindy looked me in the eye. "You tossed it aside," she said. "You don't pick it up anymore. It's not important to you now." And then without waiting for my response, she added, "That book represents the way you've treated me ever since we got married. When we were dating, you couldn't wait to pick me up. To read every page. To talk and act like I was important to your future."

I looked at my textbook in my hands, thankful I had something to look at besides her disappointed expression. "But now we're married." She pointed to her wedding ring. "And you've moved on to another semester. I'm like that book holding open your door while you walk in and do all the things that are truly important to you, I'm just not one of them."

I didn't just hear her words. I felt them. Cindy had said similar things using everyday words a hundred times before. But even when she would end our conversations with tears, it didn't emotionally move me. Then when she used a word picture – the right one for me – and I not only got it, but It also stopped me in my tracks and turned my heart in a different direction.

An emotional word picture is a communication tool that uses a story or object to simultaneously activate the emotions and intellect of the listener. In so doing, the listener experiences your words, not just hears them. In short, when you use a word picture to communicate what you're trying to convey, it can go right through your spouse's defense and straight into his or her heart.

I thought this was a great example that I just had to share. The writers go on to add there are five steps to creating emotional word pictures and share that in their book *The Language of Love*.

In the end there doesn't have to be anyone who understands you. There just has to be someone who wants to (Robert Brault).

Thank you > Love you

Yes, you say "thanks" for the big things—a gift, a foot massage, a compliment. But how about for all the little things that provide the rhythm of life? Making sure you're always stocked up on your favorite coffee? Making sure the laundry is done? A University of Georgia study found that the greatest predictor of marital quality: gratitude.

Save Up

Financial stress means your marriage will have more cracks than a chiropractor's office. Some data shows that couples with no assets are 70 percent more likely to divorce than those with at least $10,000 of assets.

Every fire needs to be stoked

Conflict isn't the only buzzkill in a marriage. The other, according to a University of Michigan study: Boredom, which makes the case for peppering your routines with some moments of unpredictability. Surprise day trips, signing up to learn a skill together, new ways to initiate a romantic tango—remember that novelty builds excitement

Control this urge

One of the most common things that happens in relationships: One person tries to change the other into doing/being better at whatever is a central issue in the relationship. "It's not that your partner will never change. It's that *you* cannot change your partner. You may support your partner in an attempt to make a change, and you may change together. For example, you both go on a diet to support one another," says **Karl Pillemer**, Ph.D, a Cornell University gerontologist, who has studied the long-term success of relationships. "But what's misguided is the idea that you can push your husband or wife to change in the direction you have chosen for him or her. People who finally accept their mate for who and what they are, rather than seeing them as a do-it-yourself project, find the experience liberating—and are much more likely to have happy and satisfying relationships for decades."

Walk before you talk

In a heated exchange because your spouse was in a third fender-bender in the last six months? Don't knee-jerk into a tirade of *what-the*'s. Give yourself a chance to calm down—so you can talk maturely to resolve the conflict. Anger is natural, but giving yourself 30 minutes before engaging can morph your argument into a discussion, which is healthier in the long-term. A UCLA study found that those who argued angrily were more likely to be divorced 10 years later than those who hashed out conflict collegially.

You will save yourself a lot of heartache if you resist the urge to publicly criticize your partner's...

Friendship is as important as love.

The secret to a long and happy marriage, according to the elders who Pillemer interviewed: "I married my best friend." Pillemer says we're schooled early on to think of friendship and romantic love as different, but what makes friendships work are the same things that make a marriage work. "We look forward to being with friends, we relish their company, we relax with them, we share common interests, and we talk openly," he says. One 87-year-old told Pillemer: "Think back to the playground when you were a child. Your spouse should be that other kid you would most like to play with!"

Never underestimate…
A kiss on the cheek.
Never underestimate…
A mid-day text just because.
Never underestimate…
What it means when your ears are "listening" and your eyes are drilled down into your phone.
Never underestimate…
Tone of voice.
It's good to regularly remind yourself of that…
Sometimes the smallest weeds poking out of the ground have the longest roots.

Address issues early

The average couple waits six years after having a relationship problem to seek some help, Bloomberg says. A counselor can help couples communicate to better fix problems before it's too late, but the key is you have to go when your relationship engine light goes on—not after you break down on the side of the road.

Don't force the "couples" thing

One of my friends said his father passed along this wisdom: "Don't expect your good friends' spouses to necessarily be good friends with your spouse. And don't expect that you're going to be buddies with your spouse's friends' spouses. Sometimes it works out that way, and that's great, but it's okay that it normally doesn't work that way."

Take the passion out of money fights

No matter your income level or assets, it's important to have some kind of third-party financial planner or counselor, who can help you work on common goals, settle disagreements, and take the emotion out of an often highly charged issue—and one that's one of the main causes of marital problems (<u>one survey</u> showed that 20 percent of people hide major transactions from their partners).

Privacy matters

Parenting decisions and sex have one thing in common: behind closed doors, always.

Celebrate small victories

Research shows that when couples whoop it up a bit when one person has even minor successes, that's good for the relationship.

Pray together, stay together

<u>A Harvard study</u> shows that married couples who attend religious services regularly are 47 percent less likely to get divorced.

Limit your social media time

There's nothing wrong with staying connected and using your various social media platforms (disclaimer: unless it's in the Tinder genre). But if you're constantly using your thumbs to click, like, and post at the expense of connecting with THE PERSON RIGHT IN FRONT OF YOU WHOM YOU HAVE PLEDGED YOUR ETERNAL COMMITMENT, it can mean trouble. <u>One survey</u> found that couples who don't use social media are 11 percent happier than those who do. (But feel free to share this story on your social networks.)

Raising Children

The difference I see with OJT (on the job training) in marriage is we've never done it when we first get married. However, we were all once children, so OJT takes on a whole different meaning. We've been there, done that. We thought our parents did some things wrong and some things right. Probably if we're honest as time goes on we'd admit they did more things right than we thought. I'd imagine this goes for every generation.

    I had a good job that allowed my wife to be a stay-at-home mom. This put much of the child raising responsibility on her. I was around the boys three or four hours per night while she was 24/7. I see so much of this has changed now. I know in the early year's kids are happy with boxes while we shower them with all sorts of gifts. I truly believe love for a child is spelled T I M E. I'm trying to get this right as a grandparent. It's great that we're given a second chance to improve on this aspect of our lives.

    A couple issues I'll share on the topic I've learned after my kids were raised but made great sense to me so I'd like to pass along. I heard two similar talks by two different parents on the subject of allowance. In a nutshell both were against it 100%. The term basically implies hand out. Instead their suggestion was to make a mini economic system inside the home. There are chores to be done, each with a set amount of pay. Younger children get less pay and easier chores and vice versa.

    One couple explained on Saturday it was payday. All chores were paid and children were taught a simple envelope system. One envelope was for saving, one for spending, and one for sharing. There were some rules, but they explained some lessons learned, sometimes the hard way. One example was children may buy something an adult would perceive as junk, but sometimes the best lessons are learned this way.

In addition, they allocated extra money for school clothes. The money would be spent regardless, but by giving the children responsibility they found they took care of their clothes, hanging them up etc. One child may want designer clothes, therefore having to wash twice per week, while another is ok with bargains and they see how much further their money goes. They mentioned how other parents were asking, "What do you do differently in raising your kids?" after a sleepover seeing such a difference in maturity. These lessons start at home. The father added how much better it is to teach children financial responsibility at an early age. Then being able to observe and give guidance while they are home, rather than turning them loose when going to college or out on their own and hoping they figure it out. Better to make a $100 mistake early on, then $1,000's later.

In addition to finance, civility can be taught in the home. No one wants to be around arguing. I heard of a family that had a family meeting and together made a list of family rules. They explained laws or rules exist for our own safety so just as we have laws outside the home, we need them inside. They made them easy one-word rules, like peace, sharing, respect, etc. Then as a family they decided on consequences when the rules were broken. Because the kids had a say in making the rules, the parents were astonished in how well they governed themselves. One example of a penalty for arguing was the two parties had to sit on a wooden bench they named the repenting bench. They had to sit there until both could decide on what their part was in the disagreement and admit it to the other, then give a hug. This applied to the parents as well.

The family meeting is a concept that never occurred to me when I was a parent to young children, but I wish I had known about it. People support what they help create. This goes for children too. Imagine the feeling a child would get if they saw their parents including them in decision making. They would most likely feel valued, loved, and included in the decision-making process.

Recently I've read articles and tips on the Ziglar web page. Zig Ziglar was instrumental in my personal development. Since he's passed away his family has done a great job in maintaining, and in some cases, further improving the material. Much of the information is free.

Mark Timm and his wife share their own advice as well as the advice of others. Two articles that stood out, and relate to the content of this chapter, include advice around family meetings and cell phone use.

Benefits of Family Meetings: (Oct 8 Ziglar Family Meetings)

1) Allows everyone to get on the same page
2) Gets rid of surprises
3) Enjoy sharing
4) We laugh at ourselves
5) We find agreement on key decisions
6) We spotlight and reward good behavior

The second article was about cell phones. When to give them, should you give them? Again, they share their thoughts and what they learned and more importantly what they'd do differently if they were to do it over again. In a nutshell they picked an age far into the future and the kids held them accountable. The day gets there quicker than you think it will. They made some rules about how the device was to be used. Though these were issues I didn't have to deal with when I was parenting adolescent children, I can see many positive things that can come out of having a plan in place. Boundaries need to be set up front. Their piece of advice for doing over was considering a family phone. Therefore no one child had their own, thus privacy issues etc. This would be dependent on how many children you had and how close in age they were.

If by the time you are reading this you realize you've done some things wrong and wonder if it's possible to repair them, the good news is YES. Regardless of what's happened we can all begin anew. We're human, we'll make mistakes, but we can learn from them and enjoy better times ahead.

Two examples I'll share on this came from the book *A Million Miles in a Thousand Years* by Donald Miller.

The first example is of a father who was on his daughter's case about her choice of a boyfriend. He could see how she was being manipulated and it concerned him for what lay ahead. He realized he hadn't provided a better role for his daughter. He hadn't mapped out a story for his family. And so, his daughter had chosen another story in which she was wanted, even if she was being used. He decided to stop yelling at her and, instead, created a better story to invite her into. Eventually she broke up with her boyfriend. He concluded; no girl who plays the role of a hero dates a guy who uses her. She knows who she is, she just forgot for a little while.

The second example was of a father/daughter relationship that had deteriorated over time as she grew older and became more interested in girl things. She and her mom had been shopping for and purchased a new dress. The daughter modeled it for her dad as he was watching SportsCenter. He said she looked nice but after thanking him, he knew he should have said more. He wanted to tell her she was beautiful and that she was his princess and all the stuff fathers find so hard to tell their daughters. He continued to watch television but couldn't get rid of that feeling. Finally, he got up from his chair, turned off the tv, went to his closet and put on his suit. He got a camera and knocked on the door. His daughter was still in her dress and he asked his wife to take their picture. He said he wanted to look good for such a special occasion. The three of them danced until one in the morning and talked about their prom days and how they wished they'd have known each other then. A great memory.

Earlier in the chapter I mentioned the book *The Five Love Languages*. Author Chapman explains children too have a primary and secondary love language. In an interview from Focus on the Family: A father arrives home, his four-year-old daughter immediately grabs his hand and wants him to accompany her to her room to show him what she's been working on all day. This is an example of the love language, quality time.

Later the father gives his six-year-old son a rock that he picked up while taking a walk during his lunch hour. He explains, I saw this today and when the sun struck it, it had the most spectacular sparkle, I thought of you. You can rest assured if the boy's primary love language is "gifts", he will still have that rock when he is 25.

Another book on parenting I'd recommend is *Have a New Kid by Friday*, written by Kevin Leman. He makes a point that if we as parents make our kids the center of the universe, be it in our speech or our actions, what room will they have for God? Too many of us want our children to be happy as a final goal. Happiness however is a byproduct of a productive, successful life. Deep down we have to realize that happiness is meaningless if we have never had unhappiness in our lives. It's similar to enjoying springtime and summer in Ohio, after experiencing winter.

You'll know what kind of a parent you were once your kids have kids and see how they do.

Parents are very important in the development of children. More is caught than taught. We know our children are watching, and they'll copy our actions both good and bad. If your language is foul you can bet those words will come out of the child's mouth as well. The same could be said for nearly everything, simple manners like please and thank you. Make sure you are setting a great example.

In Joel Osteen's *Become a Better You*, he shared a story of a game preserve where the baby elephant population was out of control. The people in charge decided to send several of the young elephants to another area many miles away. This area had many white rhinos who are not known to have any predators.

After a few weeks, however, they started finding white rhino carcasses. They eventually put up surveillance cameras in a hope to figure out what was going on. Sure enough young elephants had formed almost a gang concept and attacked the rhinos. Even though it's not even in the elephant's DNA to act in this manner it was reasoned that because they had no male influence (role model) they came up with this new behavior.

We'll all have reasons why we can't be around our home or kids at times but it's important to remember that they need us. They are our responsibility, and it's important to be there for them always, but especially in the early years. So much of their character is forming and most likely you don't want anyone else molding them but you.

> There's one sad truth in life I've found
> While journeying east or west
> The only folks we really wound
> Are those we love the best.
> We flatter those we scarcely know
> We please the fleeting guest
> And deal full many a thoughtless blow
> To those we love the best.
>
> Ella Wheeler Wilcox

I recall a co-worker telling me that as he and his wife were watching TV one night something was said that made them both snicker. He said his young daughter looked up at them wanting to know what was funny. He told her it wasn't for her to know just yet. She had heard the comment but let it go in one ear and out the other until she heard their response. Now she has become curious. She grabbed her phone to check it out and he told her, NO! It's not for you to understand right now!

When he shared that story I replied, I'm sure she will look into the phrase she heard as soon as you aren't around. It's the way kids are. They want to know things. Especially if a parent has told them to wait. I explained that as an older parent talking to a younger parent, if I had it over again, I would take those opportunities as they arise and make sure they were discussed, no matter how uncomfortable or unqualified I thought I was. My reasoning being, I don't want my children learning anything on the street or from who knows who, except from the people who love them the most, their parents.

I'd go so far as to suggest that as a family you watch movies together and have some discussion about the subject matter, age appropriate of course. Ask thought provoking questions. What can you teach your children before they experience it? Perhaps they never will but you'll have prepared them in the event they do. Who else would you trust that task to?

Best books I've read on this subject or people listened to
Mindset - Leadership and Self Deception - The 7 Habits - (these were all listed at the end of chapter 1 as well)

Experts I've either heard or read their material I'd suggest checking out.
Les and Leslie Parrott – Richard and Linda Eyre - Kevin Leman

If by the time you are reading this you are already married be sure you are doing all you can to make the marriage successful. You can only change yourself. But remember as you change you can impact others for the good over time.

If you aren't yet married be sure you've covered your pre-marital questions or some, what if's you've prepared as a couple. Also, if things come up from these discussions, let that be a reason to slow down. Don't go into a marriage thinking things will change with time. Many times, they will but not always for the better.

If you've not yet found that person don't let yourself become discouraged. I think the best place to be is in church, not bars or clubs. I'm not saying that just because a person goes to church, they are better, but if you meet someone at church the chances are better, you'll have a successful marriage.

Zig Ziglar shared a story about one of his granddaughters. She'd been dating a boy for a couple of years and seemed happy. She marveled at the marriage her grandparents had. Zig never counseled her on dropping her boyfriend, but she realized because he wasn't a Christian, she could never have what her grandparents had. Therefore, she ended the relationship.

Basic mistakes people make:

1. Not making their spouse the most important person in the family
2. Not realizing the impact of their actions, (more is caught, than taught)
3. Not learning how to communicate with children at the various stages of life
4. Allowing their children to learn life lessons from others (values need taught in the home)

5. Trying to make life easier for their children and depriving them from opportunities to learn

Questions to consider: On a scale of 1 – 10 with 10 being perfection how would you rate yourself in this area? ____
Consider

1. My marriage is my priority Y N
2. My spouse would rate our marriage on a scale of 1-10 ____? Anything less than a 10 needs discussion
3. Do we have a mini economic system set up for our children? Y N (no allowance)
4. We have adequate family time weekly set aside
5. We are great communicators with our children and understand the importance
6. I read what works for others and implement if possible
7. Our children know my spouse is my number one priority

My final thoughts / suggestions:

1) Raise your family in a church, the sooner the better but anytime is a good time to start.
2) Make time for each other, wife and husband, parents and children, don't use the excuse it's quality not quantity.
3) Read the book *The Five Love Languages*. I learned things as a 50-year-old that I would have never known about women otherwise. The same would apply for women understanding differences in men.
4) Check out www.touchinglives.org for excellent marriage sermons.

5. Other family websites for tips & advice www.focusonthefamily.com, www.familyfirst.net, www.allprodad.com, www.imom.com and add their pages to your favorite form of social media for updates.
6. Ask those you admire or notice qualities you'd like to possess for advice.
7. Read the book *Mindset* by Carol Dweck. There are many take-aways, especially praising children. Make sure it's for effort and not perfection.

I've got much more; my wife and I have passed our 40th year of marriage.

Concerning marriage, it wasn't always easy, but it is worth it.

Regarding raising children, we did our best. Looking back, we wish we knew then, what we know now. I've heard it said, you'll know what kind of parent you were, when you see what kind of parent your kids are.

CHAPTER 3

RELATIONSHIPS

People will forget what you said, people will forget what you did, but people will never forget how you made them feel.

For the sake of this writing, relationships are with everyone outside my immediate family. Some relationships are in existence because of our work, our spouse, our church, or hobbies. Regardless of where our relationships begin, the depth of them takes effort.

Friendship is a word that is thrown around casually this day in age. You can friend someone on Facebook and not even know them. However, there is a difference between being friendly with someone versus being a friend. Usually, we associate certain traits or qualities with a friend, things like loyalty, honesty, kindness, and trustworthiness to name a few. Consequently, we expect certain behavior from a friend versus an acquaintance. We also treat our friends differently than an acquaintance. Therefore, friendship carries both privileges and responsibilities.

I heard a speaker once say he attended a seminar where the leader asked where the responsibility lies in relationships. One attendee shouted 50/50 another said 51/49 thinking you should always give a little more. Still another shouted 80/20 without explanation. Finally, the speaker wrote on the board

100/0, and then explained that you need to put 100% effort in, without any expectation of gain.

This goes against what most of us probably think but imagine if everyone treated each other this way. We would listen to understand as opposed to waiting for the person to finish so we could get our two cents in. Have you ever considered that the words *listen* and *silent* share the same letters rearranged into a different sequence? Perhaps there's a hint in that coincidence; to be a good listener, we need to become silent. The best way to capture a person's attention is to give them all of yours.

That reminds me of a story of a woman who was a reporter. She got the chance to interview two different prominent men on consecutive days. A colleague asked her opinion of the first interview, to which she replied she was convinced he was the smartest person she'd ever met. When asked about the second gentleman she replied she thought she was the most interesting person he'd ever met. Can you guess which gentleman she favored?

Andy Andrews shared wisdom that has stuck with me and I'd like to pass along. So, what is a friend, a true friend? When that question was asked time and again the number one response was, "someone who accepts me as I am". His response, the guy at the drive thru window accepts you as you are! A friend, a true friend would hold me to a higher standard. They'll call me out when that's needed and encourage me when I'm on track. They won't just agree all the time. They'll make me a better person.

This particular piece of the Eight Facets of Life is not a strength of mine. In general, I'd say women are naturally better at relationships than men, although I know there are always exceptions. Women are better in that they seem to have more close personal relationships. In my work life I spent many years in a supervisory role, so I credit that to why I have a more guarded personality. However, with the people

I worked with, I've heard (more than once) that I'm much different than he/she perceived after getting to know me on a more personal level.

You Add Value to People When You Value Them

I have always tried to value people. I recall our plant manager coming to me one day and asking what I was doing differently than the other departments. He knew we had a better retention rate than anyone else and wanted to understand what was different. We had temporary associates as well as permanent ones that worked side by side. We made sure that all had the same training and were treated the same. Feeling part of the team they tended to stay longer, and many stayed until an opportunity to be hired came along.

At one point the economy took a turn, and I had the unpleasant task of releasing all of our temporary associates. To make matters worse it was nearing Christmas. I could have had their immediate supervisors tell them, but I had a better plan. I approached a cleaning contractor that I had developed a relationship with who was a key supplier to our department. I knew he had regular turnover and suggested he interview those associates who had shown their reliability by having perfect attendance for multiple years. He enthusiastically agreed.

I don't recall anyone taking me up on our offer but many expressed appreciation in the fact we made an effort to find them employment. The slowdown didn't last long and in a short time most came back to work with us, knowing we valued them.

In the book *The 01 Minute Manager* by by Spencer Johnson and Kenneth H. Blanchard, "Everyone is a potential winner, some are disguised as losers. Don't let their appearance fool you." I recall a guy I worked with that was reluctant to use the computer. I asked others that knew him better why that might be? They all said, "You'll never change _____." I approached him one day and asked if he saw any reason not to learn? He said there was just no need. I showed him some basic uses from a personal side, then asked if he could see how, it might be applied to make his work more efficient. Immediately he came up with some. It wasn't a big deal, but it opened up new opportunities and expanded his world.

A similar situation came up a few years later in another department. We had an employee who everyone said would never be able to do the job because he was computer illiterate. Having had past success, I was determined to prove them wrong. I worked with him, and eventually he became proficient. As I mentioned, everyone is a potential winner, even though some are disguised as losers. They might be disguised in such a way because they are lacking in some technical skill or even because of a bad attitude. I worked with a company after retirement on some training they wanted everyone in their company to go through. The topic was "Teamwork." I had completed a couple sessions and before the next group arrived, I was warned by HR and another manager that a guy was coming in that would most likely be troublesome. I thanked them for their concern and aforementioned warning but felt I'd be able to handle the situation.

Sure, enough the guy had something to say. Luckily for me he was the first to arrive. He advised me that he wasn't too excited to be here, and that he didn't go for this type of stuff. He likes to do his job and go home. I suggested he listen to what I'd prepared and was welcome to add if he felt compelled to do so. Otherwise, I'd welcome his opinion afterwards.

I began the training and it lasted about an hour and a half. Some comments were made but nothing negative. The gentleman I'd been warned about made sure he was the last to leave. He approached me and we shook hands. He thanked me for coming and said a lot of what I shared made sense and he was going to change some things in his life. I have no idea if he did or if he meant personally or professionally, but I felt good about myself and the message I had delivered. I rarely, if ever, give up on another human being. This is an example of why we shouldn't.

Evaluating your associations - No road is long with good company. Turkish proverb

In the book *The 12 Pillars* by Jim Rohn and Chris Widener, there is a chapter devoted to relationships. The authors recommended evaluating your friends into 3 categories: 1) dissociation 2) limited association 3) expanded association. Dissociation refers to the friends who are pulling you down or holding you back. Limited association refers to friends who are ok to be around, but not all day or too frequently. Expanded association refers to friends who make you better, draw out your best, push, encourage, challenge. These are the people who we need to be around, and if we become better at noticing, will attract into our lives.

Many parents are concerned about who their children are around. Parents understand that bad behavior can rub off on their children, but at what age does that not become a factor? Answer, never! That's why we need to be around the best people we know, or the best we can find. If you ask a friend (who you consider exceptional) if they would be willing to meet with you periodically, most likely they would say yes. They would be flattered. If you do go this route, be sure you are prepared. Tell them exactly what you admire about them. If you meet them for coffee or lunch, offer to pick up the tab. Come with a list of questions, don't settle for idle chit chat. This will show them you are serious, and value their time. Usually a monthly or bi-monthly meeting is enough. Don't ask for more than that. Realize they have responsibilities as well. Take notes so you'll remember but also to show them how serious you are about learning.

Ben Franklin

It's been said that Benjamin Franklin had a great method for becoming a better person that he credited to his overall success. Others have adopted this method as well, including investor, business tycoon, and philanthropist Warren Buffet. He says to imagine a person that you really admire. Write their name on a piece of paper. Now write everything about them that you admire. It could be their positive self-talk, the way they never seem to get upset, the way they treat others, or a hundred other things. The key is to be specific and write a lot.

Then write the names of people you'd rather not be around. Do the same exercise, but ask yourself why not? Write and write a lot. Again, it could be they don't treat others with respect, always like to have the last word. Maybe they won't let others speak or share an opinion. Again, the sky's the limit regarding what qualities you don't like.

Once you have those two lists, people you admire, and people you don't, simply work every day on the traits you admire and make sure you aren't acting like those you don't.

Of the Eight Facets, I'd considered combining family and relationships into one category. However, the more I considered it, the more I came to the conclusion that family was too personal and relationships were too big. Life is built around interaction with others. Even if you are a private, keep to yourself kind of person, you still need to come out of your shell from time to time. In fact, I've found that when this type of person speaks, others take notice, because they aren't talking all the time.

I heard a fascinating story recently about lightning bugs. The speaker explained a lightning bug has two purposes: to eat for survival and to mate. We have all seen them, and likely spent some time catching them in our youth. One thing I remember is how they light up and you'd move in that direction only to lose track of where it flew. Another lights up, you chase it, and the night goes on. It was only when I would sit back and watch that I would see a pattern. If you move about the yard with a little more purpose, it almost seemed like they would come right to you. Throughout the night they would light up, then another, and another.

Science tells us that the male is sending out his light to attract a female. They also speculate that the odds of finding a mate is around 3%.

Now for the fascinating part. A researcher was canoeing a river in Indonesia. As he proceeded down the river and the night fell, he came upon a tree that literally lit up simultaneously. It was as if someone flipped a switch. A few seconds later it did it again. And then to his amazement for the next 100 yards the same thing was happening in every tree. These lightning bugs were timing their pulses in synchronization.

When he returned to the United States and told his story no one believed him. Biologists said it was impossible, mathematicians said it was impossible. But it was true. They argued why they wouldn't light up at the same time, when the purpose of lighting up was to stand out and find a mate.

Later MIT did an experiment with LED lights and found that when pulses are timed to the millisecond the likelihood of the bugs finding a mate was 82%. Remember it was only 3% by themselves. The bugs had figured out that by synchronizing their pulses they attracted more females to the area, millions more.

This phenomenon happens in only 2 places in the world. Indonesia and Elkmont, Tennessee.

The world tells us its survival of the fittest. It's a dog-eat-dog world. This is similar to a person who believes there is only so much to go around. It's a scarcity mindset versus an abundance mindset. I like the philosophy of a rising tide floats all ships. I think that's what the lightning bugs figured out, by working together they've improved their likelihood of success by 79%. Mankind needs to adopt this ourselves. Don't think about being brighter than anyone, but let your light magnify with others to let the world see.

During World War II, enemies torpedoed a Navy cruiser carrying more than 1,100 crewmembers. As the ship sank into the frigid water, the crew floundered in the sea for five days. They were starving, drowning, and being attacked by sharks. The ocean current pulled nine of the men away from the others. Seeing these men were beginning to lose their will, a young officer started asking them about their families and lives back home. He asked them to describe what they were going to do when they got back. He asked them what they wanted to accomplish and what difference they wanted to make.

He had them envision how scared their spouses and children were; how their parents must feel not knowing if they were alive. He asked them to fight to stay alive, not just for themselves but for their loved ones back home. Finally, a passing plane spotted the men in the water. Two-thirds of the 1,100 crew members perished. However, all nine who were encouraged by that young officer lived.

Hopefully we'll never have to experience anything like this. However, can you see how one person can make a difference? By offering encouragement and helping the men realize it was not just about them, most likely gave these men a reason to hang on.

Social investment is one of the main attributes for success. I've read several books that have indicated those with deeper relationships do better in almost every aspect of life. They live longer, they earn more, they live overall happier lives. I think I first heard this from Jim Rohn when he claimed that your personality is formed from traits of the five people you are around the most. If this is true it applies to earnings, hobbies, marriage, kids etc. If a close friend gets a divorce the likelihood that you may go up 300%. If your friends are overweight, chances go up considerably that you will be as well.

That's why you want to choose your friends wisely. Look for people that are successful in all that you want to attain. It may not be one person that is successful at everything and most likely won't be. For instance, you may admire the way someone Is always pleasant. A genuine smile, having never heard them say anything bad about anyone. Perhaps they've even stopped a conversation that headed that way. Another person seems to have raised their children in a manner that shows complete respect to their parents and others. Another seems to have had a successful business career or overcome a health problem. It would be wise to seek these people out and spend as much time as possible with them. There's a good chance you'll learn something. If by chance you discover things aren't as they appear that's okay too. You take the good you can learn and apply it, while leaving the poor habits.

> You can kiss your family and friend's good-bye and put miles between you, but at the same time you carry them with you in your heart, your mind, your stomach, because you do not just live in a world but a world lives in you. (Fredrick Buechner)

> Some people come into our lives and quickly go. Some stay for a while, leave footprints on our hearts, and we are never, ever the same again. (Flavia Weedn)

A closing poem from John Wooden
At times when I am feeling low,
I hear from a friend and then
My worries start to go away
And I am on the mend.
In spite of all that doctors know,
And their studies never end,
The best cure of all when spirits fall
Is a kind note from a friend.

Think of a football team and you are the quarterback. On the offensive side the quarterback is the key player, everything starts with him. Think of yourself as the key player of your life, because you are. Everything starts with you. The offensive line is made up of five players that are usually bigger in size that serve as protection to the quarterback. The offensive line is your equivalent of your relationships. These are people who should only be there for your benefit. The benefit is that they are looking out for your best interest, helping you become better, pointing out areas that you could improve in. Likewise, you may be the equivalent of that same to the other person's offensive line. As a matter of fact, relationships need to be a two-way street. Surrounded by family and positive relationships, big challenges feel more manageable and small challenges don't even register on your radar. Our social ties help us capitalize on our strengths – to accomplish more in our work and our lives.

A great book to read to see others as people not objects, *Leadership and Self-Deception: Getting Out of the Box* by The Arbinger Institute. A friend suggested this, and I'm grateful he did. It opened my eyes about various relationships like family and business.

Assumptions are the termites of relationships. (Henry Winkler)

Relationships

I heard a man say recently that today's generation is more connected than ever before. He meant that in a good way. I wonder, though, the depth of those connections. To have friends that like posts you do on Facebook or Instagram to me doesn't say much. It doesn't take much effort to hit a "like" button.

I recall a man once proclaiming that we all need the type of relationships that if he was unfairly convicted and sentenced in a foreign jail, his friend would work to get him out. Many friends would say I'm sorry about what happened, might pray for you, or offer to come to a party the day you got released. I wonder if that's the type of relationships we are building today.

Do you remember the days you'd get a pop-in visit? I do. One of our aunts/uncles would pull in and mom would say, "Oh my, so and so is here." We'd pick things up to make the house look more presentable. The adults would gather and talk while us kids would play. At some point there would invariably be a meal put together and several hours after the pop-in, the guests would leave and we'd all be richer for the experience.

That doesn't happen anymore. It seems like we are either too busy or we are waiting for an invitation. For that reason, I'm wondering if relationships today are as meaningful as in past times?

A coworker shared something with me once as a group of us were talking about the idea of a pop-in visit. He said, "If you're coming to visit, stop anytime. If you're coming to see the house, make an appointment." I know I once showed a guy our home who stopped by. He actually asked if he could see it. I took him room by room. As we were leaving the house my wife came home, and she was a little upset with me for showing anyone because things weren't picked up like she wished they would have been. The thought never crossed my mind to run in and check things out before taking him

in. I guess because I'd never judge someone by a pillow out of place, I didn't think they would me either. Maybe that's a difference between men and women?
Basic mistakes people make:

1) Looking for a friend rather than being a friend
2) Being a true friend, holding them to a higher standard
3) Afraid of disassociation of relationships if they are toxic
4) Listening to reply/give advice instead of listening to understand.
5) Failing to surround ourselves with positive role models.

Questions to consider: On a scale of 1 – 10 with 10 being perfection how would you rate yourself in this area? ____
Consider

1) How many true friends do I have?
2) Am I being a true friend?
3) Are the people around me better because I'm there?
4) If not, what can I do to bring out the best in others? If yes, how can I help them even more?
5) Do I see others as objects, to serve me, or people?

Takeaway: People need people, find those of similar interest or those you have something in common with. Most importantly find people who will hold you accountable to becoming the best you are capable of becoming. There is a mental sharpness that comes from being around good people.

Leaders on the topic of Relationships:
Andy Andrews--American author of more than 20 self-help and advice books, including *The Traveler's Gift*.

The Seven Decisions: Understanding the Keys to Personal Success by Andy Andrews

Leadership and Self-Deception: Getting Out of the Box by The Arbinger Institute.

CHAPTER 4

HEALTH

Things left to themselves tend to deteriorate.

I'm combining fitness and health into one category mainly because I don't feel one exists without the other. Health can mean a lot of things to different people. Some people struggle with high blood pressure, another with cholesterol and on and on. Most of what I'll cover here though is weight control and fitness. I think for most people weight is the issue that makes most of our other problems materialize. I realize depending on where you are in life, and depending on your age, you may be limited by the amount of fitness you do. Not to say it should though. More on that later.

If *knowing how* were enough, we'd all be rich and thin. For example, everyone *knows* that it's unhealthy to be overweight, and yet 64% of Americans are, and an amazing 30% are technically obese according to http://www.cdc.gov/nchs/fastats/overwt.htm. Ask any group of reasonably intelligent adults for advice on how to shave off a few pounds and they will come up with some great dieting advice like, "Eat less, exercise more." It's common sense, right? Common sense, but NOT common practice.

In a 2004 documentary film Morgan Spurlock follows a non-traditional diet of McDonald's food for 30 days. He ate three meals a day and, if he was asked if he wanted to "supersize it", the answer was always yes. He had medical checks done prior and then again after 30 days. All his vital signs were significantly worse after the experiment. He gained 20 pounds or so. The message loud and clear was Fast Food is Bad for You. However, a science teacher encouraged by his students, tried a McDonald's diet too. The rules were to eat the recommended calories per day. In 30 days, he dropped several pounds and lowered his blood pressure. So, what's the difference? US.

I have always heard health is a combination of what we eat (diet) and how active we are (exercise). After many years of experience, I actually think that exercise is 25% and intake is 75%. I made exercise a major priority at one time in my life. My weight had reached 245 pounds. I graduated high school at 180 pounds. For reference, a healthy weight for me at 5'10' is 149-183 pounds according to the AMA. A man who is 5 ft. 10 in. tall is considered overweight (BMI is 25 to 29) if he weighs between about 174 and 202 pounds, and is obese (BMI is 30 or more) if he is closer to 209 pounds or more. Through my life, the pounds came on gradually--not so much the first 5 years, but then five pounds here and another five a few months later. Eventually 10 pounds turned into 20 and on and on. In your 20's and 30's you can diet and exercise and get back in shape pretty quickly. It seems, though, as we age the pounds don't come off as easily.

Once I hit the almost 250 mark, I knew I had to do something. I tried exercising after work but it seemed like there was always a reason I couldn't commit. The kids had a ball game, or I worked overtime and was too tired. Finally, I had a job change that changed my start time from 5am to 7am. I was used to getting up early so I used the extra two hours I had gained to start an exercise routine. I dropped 20 pounds in only a few months. Then winter came, and it was all I could do to maintain my weight. In the spring and summer, I would lose another 20 pounds until eventually

I had lost 50 pounds. Over the years I have maintained a similar routine. Winter is always the hardest for me and I sometimes gain 10-20 pounds depending on how uncommitted I am at the time.

Health is an area that I feel is probably as neglected as any. The main reason, we think we can always get serious about it **tomorrow**. The cheeseburger we eat, or any sweets, or high calorie drinks won't kill us today. Therein lies the problem. It's so easy to put off. The problem, however, is poor choice after poor choice adds up. It should be easy to change our ways. The problem is, it's also easy *not* to change our ways.

I heard a story of a man who was several hundred pounds overweight. He claimed to have tried everything. If he had any loss it seemed in a few weeks he'd gain it back and then some. His daughter had a health problem and needed a transplant. He was the only match. Doctors however wouldn't allow him to go through with the surgery until he lost well over a hundred pounds. He did it many months in advance of the plan. When asked how he explained, "I never had a big enough why. When my *why* was bigger than my *but*, it was simple."

Probably more has been written on health than any other of the *Eight Facets*. Research has been done and results shared time and again that contradict each other. At one time we were told to limit eggs or don't even eat them. Today they are considered an excellent health source. The same with milk, at one time it was a staple of the American diet, especially for children. Now it's come under fire for many health problems.

It seems that any tested diet is at one time deemed to be good for us, only to be retested and deemed bad for us. Alternatively, we could study health ourselves and after digesting the information come to our own conclusion. It's not to say we'll be running laboratory tests but we can make a journal and document how we feel after eating certain foods as well as our activity, much like how elimination diets and food allergy testing work.

In addition, I'd be leery of who I listen to for health advice. Just because it worked for cousin Eddie, doesn't mean he had the same issues you do, so no guarantee it will work for you. Celebrities pitch a new diet routinely as well as well-meaning friends and family. Again, look for long term results. If aunt Lucy lost 20 pounds on the crispy crème diet in three months, I'd like to see how she's doing a year and even two years down the road. It seems like everyone wants to share what worked for them and how easy it was, and how much better they feel. If it's true, great, just remember long term results are the proof. We didn't get into our situation overnight; most likely we won't improve it overnight either.

A few tips I'll share that seem common sense to me:

Water:

If our bodies are made up of 70% water, it stands to reason that water intake should be a priority. Also, the water should be clean and free of anything harmful. *The Seven Pillars of Health* by Dr. Don Colbert shares that the FDA administers policy on food whereas the EPA does so for water. Many of the bottled waters aren't what they appear to be.

You've probably heard of the Dead Sea before. It's in the Middle East and has the name because it has water running into it, but nothing running out. In addition, it is the saltiest water on earth. If there isn't flow in and out, it isn't fit for fish and plant life. Much like our bodies if we aren't taking in enough water our bodies can't flourish.

Our brains often mistake the signals of thirst as hunger. The next time you want a snack, try drinking a glass of water, then wait 15 minutes and see if that does the trick.

Additionally, I read an article recently that said our body percentage of water decreases as we age. As a one-year-old our body is 86% water, dropping to 75% as a 5–14-year-old. Then to 65% at age 20-35, 55% age 40-50 and finally to 50% at age 60 and beyond. Just the fact we are made of such a high percentage at all ages should tell us we need to stay hydrated and flush our bodies regularly like the example of the dead sea mentioned earlier.

The benefits of staying hydrated include, fatigue buster, aids muscle function, blood normalizer, brain booster, productivity booster, it aids digestion, improves skin appearance, waste remover and assists with calorie control.

Sleep:
Sleep is crucial to our body. Many people deprive themselves of sleep saying they are too busy to get everything done and sleeping less is the only alternative. When we fail to get the proper sleep, our body can't repair itself as it was designed to.

I heard a doctor once explain that just as an office needs cleaning so does our body. He said to think of it like a cleaning team comes to the building and empties waste baskets, vacuums the carpets, mops the floor and washes the windows. Our bodies are doing the same thing while we sleep. This is provided we give it ample time to do so as well as eat healthy and drink plenty of water. When we deprive ourselves the needed rest, we pay for it in the long run.

We pay for it by: fatigue, memory issues, mood changes, weakened immunity, trouble with thinking and concentration, weight gain, and many preventable diseases.

Once we are fatigued it affects the brain in many detrimental ways. I know I went through a period of not getting enough sleep and it led to an auto accident. Thankfully no one was hurt as I went off the side of the road and hit a guardrail but that incident awakened me to the necessity of getting proper sleep.

Nutrition:
Nutrition comes mainly in the form of the food we eat. If you don't care for certain foods that you know are healthy

don't assume you'll always maintain the taste you have. Our brains are good at creating habits. Any consistent and repetitive choice can become a new habit. I've read we can change our brains to crave healthier foods through repetition. It might take a while but choices like this can go a long way to creating a healthier you.

I'm getting that way with broccoli. I keep trying cauliflower and am not there yet but I keep trying. The longer you can stick with a healthier diet, the more your brain will crave those foods.

Supplements:

Since 90% of us aren't eating right and the foods we eat aren't as nutritious as they were in the past it stands to reason we should take vitamins. What you take should be recommended by your doctor after taking a physical. This is an area I've failed to take seriously but have since done after reading more material. My logic was I didn't trust that a pill could make up for my poor eating habits. My thinking was they could put anything in there and who would know the difference? However, I recently heard a friend say that his doctor told him his kidney stones could likely come from taking vitamins that his body didn't need. Another case of what's good for one person might not be good for everyone.

Additionally, an article I read trying to research vitamins done by the Cleveland Clinic said that taking vitamins showed no increase in life expectancy. So again, the more you read and research the more confused you may become. I'd say do your own research and monitor how you feel and your body reacts. Then you can decide.

Exercise

It's been said you can't out exercise a bad diet. I'd have to agree with that because I feel like I tried. No one worked out any harder than I did when I got committed around the age of 45. However, by not making correct diet choices my weight still fluctuated greatly.

Many trainers give the advice of mixing strength training and aerobic activity into your weekly exercise routine. Different trainers will suggest different ratios and types of activity based on your age, condition, and what you have access to. With your doctor's approval, you should try a program that meets your needs and excites you. After some time, you may need to adjust or tweak your plan as necessary.

When you begin a new program, you might be sore if your body isn't used to it. Start slowly and keep going. As I write this, I've just attempted to get back into exercising regularly, and my legs are quite sore. That didn't stop me from doing 30 minutes of activity this morning, and once finished, I felt much better.

Sitting is the new smoking; we are killing ourselves with inactivity and poor diets. In some parts of the world, a good portion of the community spends much of their waking hours moving. Whether they walk to work or live in a place where the weather is mostly sunny and warm, people are more likely to be moving around than sitting down. Likewise, diets around the world are pretty different. For example, many Mediterranean dishes are full of healthy fats and fresh produce. It is in some of these communities, where exercise and healthy diets are considerably better, that people tend to live longer lives.

Additionally, exercise, especially aerobic exercise is linked to better brain health. When we exercise and get our heart rates up the blood pumping has been proven to assist with moods, and delaying brain diseases like dementia and Alzheimer's.

Detox Baby Steps

Diet Tips

1) Drink lots of water - Sometimes thirst can be confused with hunger, therefore drinking water first may make you feel less hungry.

2) Be careful about nighttime snacks – Many times sitting in front of the tv we get caught up in mindless eating. Limit it to something light like air popped popcorn or a 100-calorie pack of something you enjoy.

3) Don't avoid your favorite foods altogether - Moderation is key. If you enjoy candy bars, have a mini bar occasionally rather than the full size.

4) Have snacks if needed – This is debated by some, but many times if you feel hungry and deprive yourself, you'll overeat at meal time. Some health experts recommend eating five small meals per day. If you try this method and find that your meal sizes are appropriate--you feel satiated and are maintaining a healthy lifestyle--this might be a good plan for you! If you try this method and find that you are still reaching for too many snacks between meals, you may reconsider this plan. If you go the five small meal routes just monitor your results and make sure the calories are reasonable.

5) Eat protein at every meal – Protein provides energy and keeps you feeling full longer. Protein is also important for muscle mass. Meats, seafood, eggs, nuts, beans and yogurt are good sources of protein.

6) Watch portion sizes – You can even order children's portions or senior portions when dining out. Some people use smaller plates.

7) Eat breakfast – Again this might not be for you. I never feel hungry when I wake up. My best health period I worked out after waking up, then ate something like oatmeal afterwards. Once a week I'd treat myself to eggs, sausage and toast as well. Some experts disagree with this. Decide what works for you.

8) Fiber – Fiber has many health benefits. It helps with digestion, lowers cholesterol levels, and prevents constipation. Fiber also makes you feel full. Beans, whole grains, vegetables and fruits are good sources of fiber.

9) Lose weight slowly – Losing one to two pounds per week is considered the optimal pace for keeping the weight off. Most of us want it to happen more quickly, and it can, but it's usually not sustainable. Health benefits begin when we lose five to ten percent of our body weight.

10) Weigh-ins – Some experts recommend daily weigh-ins, some weekly. You will no doubt fluctuate day to day, so keep that in mind if you do it daily. Don't get discouraged. Be consistent on the time of day you weigh-in and make sure you use the same scale.

11) Get plenty of sleep – A lack of sleep is thought to lead to a bigger appetite. You will feel healthier and fuller if you get adequate sleep.

12) Eat more fruit and vegetables – Fruits and vegetables should be a focus in your nutrition as they are typically high in water and fiber.

13) Keep a food diary – Writing down what you eat makes you more aware of what, how much, and when you are eating. Usually that leads to reduced calories.

14) Celebrate success – Just not with food. Reward yourself with an activity or reasonable purchase.

15) Get help if needed – Some people need a workout buddy. If that's you go for it. Many times, you can get assistance from a trainer where you work out.

Eight months out of the year I play golf. I always walk a hilly course, and that seems to suffice along with the other outdoor activity I do to maintain my health. However, the other four months I need to add some aerobic activity along with less intake than I allow myself in the summer.

I was talking to a nutritionist this past week and asked her about skipping meals and/or fasting. She said there are so many theories on the subject. One thing she mentioned was if we fast, only to indulge later, we've achieved nothing, and perhaps done more harm. However, if you aren't hungry, it's perfectly ok to miss a meal. Some experts actually suggest 16 hour fasts periodically. It seems similar to studies on diets that say don't eat eggs or dairy, then later the advice is reversed to say eat lots of eggs and don't skimp on dairy. It's no wonder there is confusion. The nutritionist's advice: be sensible, eat lots of vegetables, and fruits. What works for one person is no guarantee it will work for you.

The diet industry is a multibillion-dollar market. It amazes me to see celebrities who get to pitch their product, only to have them gain it back and then some. The fact is nothing will work unless we do.

I had a trainer tell me that the standards that doctors use for suggested body weights for men and women were based on studies done many decades ago. Researchers assessed people who lived into their eighties and up and determined that if these people outlived others, their weights must be optimal. He then added that by those standards, every male trainer that works here is obese. Those trainers were more concerned with blood pressure, resting heart rate, waist size, BMI, etc.

The fact is everyone has an opinion of what you should do. The only opinion that matters is yours and your trusted medical professional. Do you want better health? I've heard the best time to plant a tree was 20 years ago. The next best time is today. The same could be said about our health. It would be great to have started years ago or even last month. Don't let that stop you anymore. Today is the first day of the rest of your life. Make it a day your future self with thank you for. Is your *why* bigger than your *but*? The truth is few things are more important than our health. Without it, enjoying the good things in life can be hard. Unfortunately, many people aren't motivated to care about their health until after they discover problems. By then it may be too late.

Although regular exercise and eating a balanced and nutritious diet can't guarantee a healthy future, these habits will certainly go a long way to preventing many of the most common causes of death and or disease. Taking precautionary measures like regular check-ups and other suggested tests help as well by detecting problems early.

A few more tips, if you don't do cardio and strength train while losing weight, 25 percent of every pound you lose will come from lean calorie burning muscle.

> what you eat is just as important as how much you consume
> resist the impulse to go for the fast fix. Most transformations take months or years of sustained effort
> adjust your workouts as your weight loss progresses for lasting results
> make a goal but be willing to adjust. Also look at the progress and not the gap
> if you lower your calories by 30% eventually your metabolism will slow by 30%

Health

Try HIT (high intensity interval training), going hard for a moment then easier. On an elliptical you can accomplish with the random workout; on a bike I ride hard for a minute followed by a more relaxed pace for a minute and alternate throughout

In summary, educate yourself and make it a priority to maintain a healthy lifestyle. You'll be of little value to anyone if you don't feel well. There is so much information out there, make sure you take the time to educate yourself then most importantly act on what you learn.

I listened to some podcasts recently that talked alot about health and especially nutrition. The idea of fasting and the benefits that have when done. Some health experts advise a daily fast of 12-16 hours allowing your body to digest the foods and do its job of cleansing and digesting. Some also suggest periodically doing a 2-3 day fast in addition. If you try those however be sure you read about the things to be on the lookout for. Also, if you have any health conditions be sure to consult your doctor before trying anything.

Diet is an area that experts can't agree on. I have listened to both JJ Virgin and Jillian Michaels audiobooks. Both are considered experts but seem to contradict each other. One says it's just calories in and calories out. The other said their pet peeve was when so-called experts say it's just calories in and calories out. Both of these women are considered health experts and have huge followings. Yet their advice on diet is 180 degrees in the opposite direction.

Don't blame the so-called experts. It's your life, do something today that your future self will thank you for.

I've listened to a podcast with Jon Gordon who I'd primarily classify as a personal development expert but he has shared what's worked in his life as well. A couple podcasts I recall were doctors he had thought highly of and had them share their work. I'd highly recommend listening to it.

They were Dr. Christian Gonzalez, Dr. Joseph Maroon and a woman health expert Lauren Mones who discussed gut health and its impact on our overall health.

This comment isn't a jab at doctors but I've come to believe that our bodies can heal themselves much of the time. I think drugs are prescribed too quickly but then again maybe that's what the majority of people want is the quick fix without too much effort.

A couple of other YouTube videos I'd recommend with regard to healing yourself were from psychologist Alia Crum at a Ted X Talk at Traverse City as well as Dr Lissa Rankin a talk labeled healing yourself. They cite some amazing examples of the body doing just that.

Kevin Miller also has a podcast I've been listening to that discusses health. He actually hosts three different ones but True Life is one that is specific to health. I think you would be glad you tried it out.

Zig Ziglar once told a story about a man that owned many prize racehorses. He had educated himself on everything a horse needed to be its best. Everything from nutrition to exercise. His horses had the best trainers and best nutrition. Yet the owner of these prize race horses was a heavy smoker and at least 50 pounds overweight. The speaker's point was, how could a person be so educated and committed to a horse and yet not be an example of health himself? Perhaps before we judge the man in that story, though, we need to look at ourselves. We have a vast number of books and research on the subject of health, but many of us treat today as any other day. We know we should do something but why not get started tomorrow? Sadly, tomorrow is not guaranteed to anybody.

Basic mistakes people make:

1) Mistaking hunger for thirst

2) Not getting enough sleep
3) Not drinking enough water
4) Not exercising and not realizing the consequences
5) Not maintaining healthy habits, balanced eating, moving, preventive health care
6) Not working out hard enough/ pushing yourself
7) Lack of meal planning, which can lead to unwise food grabs.

Questions to consider: On a scale of 1 – 10 with 10 being perfection how would you rate yourself in this area? ____
Consider

1) Do I know my key numbers? weight, BMI, Blood pressure, cholesterol
2) If I need to make changes, am I willing to?
3) Do I drink enough water?
4) Do I get enough sleep?
5) Have I had a physical recently?

Takeaway:

- Make yourself get active: pick an activity and stick with it.
- Pick days and times you can commit to exercising on a regular basis.
- Studies show working out with a partner is best but I've overcome that so don't let that become an excuse.
- Exercise has been proven to stimulate the brain and affect every other body part as well. I can vouch for that, some of my best ideas come to me during a workout.

- I feel my best when I've pushed myself through a workout. Hitting the shower is a sense of accomplishment, and in my case, starting my day with exercise made all the difference to tackle the day's problems. It's exhilarating-- get started.
- Work to maintain a balanced diet, including trying new foods and keeping sweets to a minimum.
- Think of food as fuel, not a social activity.
- Beware of mindless eating, this is especially true when we eat in front of the tv.
- Keep hydrated and drink lots of water, because sometimes we mistake thirst for hunger.
- Think of your body as an instrument, not an ornament!
- Tell yourself, "I'm not on a diet, I'm just holding myself accountable for what I eat."
- Dr. Oz claims that if you were only going to make one health change, get enough sleep.
- If you are ever around someone who has had a heart attack don't stop chest compressions just because there is no pulse. I've heard doctors claim that if oxygen stops to the brain there is little hope but that is what compressions do. I learned this from a CPR class
- Lastly if someone isn't breathing but they've been underwater, especially cold water there is hope so don't give up. I've heard of people being in cold water for several minutes and surviving

There are many great websites that have free advice on health and nutrition. Magazines often have websites with at least some of the information free. Also check out the library for books, magazines, and exercise videos.

Best material on this subject:

The Seven Pillars of Health by Don Colbert
Weekly newsletter www.threedimensionalvitality.com
    Ann Musico a trusted resource I read regularly. backs up her opinions with much research
You Tube checkout Dr Eric Berg

CHAPTER 5

CAREER

*Choose a job you love,
and you will never have to work a day in your life.*
-Confucius

Career--What is it?

To me, a career means the various jobs I had during my working years. A quick search on Google suggests that a career is an individual's journey through learning, work and other aspects of life. For the purpose of this chapter, it's what you do work-wise to earn money.

For most of us we'll spend more time on this aspect of our life than any other, maybe more here than the other seven combined. No doubt you've heard of some people who make their life their work.

I think our work is a vital component to our well-being. It contributes to our sense of self-worth. Society places more glamour on some positions or well-paying jobs, but to me the main objective is to find work you enjoy and put your heart into it.

In a college graduation speech, I read about the speaker Edward James Olmos. He was an actor who played Jamie Escalante in the movie *Stand and Deliver*. He advised the graduates to never work for money. He stressed please don't just go get a job. A job is something you do for money but a career is something you do because you're inspired to do it. You want to do it, you love doing it, you're excited when you do it.

I've seen people go for interviews and simply consider what is the salary when making their choice. There are so many more things to consider. What about benefits? Retirement may not be a big consideration when you are 20, but it's important when you are 50. Consider everything that is being offered in addition to salary. The company I worked for had never had a layoff in over 50 years of existence, and although that can't be a future guarantee, it sure sounded appealing to anyone who wanted security.

Aside from the money and benefits, another important consideration to make is *what am I going to be doing?* Will it be challenging and rewarding? Will I have the ability to make a difference and grow with the company? These are some of the main reasons people list for leaving a job, not money.

Olmos concluded his speech with these words, "Chase your passion, not your pension! Be inspired to learn as much as you can, to find a cause that benefits mankind, and you'll be sought after for your quality of service and dedication to excellence. This passion will make you oblivious of quitting time and the length of your workday. You'll awake everyday with the passion of pursuit, but not the pursuit of money."

Those who do more than they are paid for are always sought for their services. Their name and work will outlive them and always command the highest wage. Chase your passion and not your pension! A faculty member was heard to say, "Maybe we should have taught that in class."

James Michener says the following about work:

> *The master in the art of living makes little distinction between his work and his play, his labor and his leisure, his mind and his body, his information and his recreation, his love and his*

religion. He hardly knows which is which. He simply pursues his vision of excellence at whatever he does, leaving others to decide whether he is working or playing. To him he is always doing both.

Is work that necessary evil that consumes the time between our brief periods of enjoyment on the weekends? Is it primarily a method of paying the bills and showing responsibility? Or a way to prove to your parents that the college degree was a reasonable investment? Or the shortest path to retirement? Or is it more?

In the book The *Millionaire Mind by Thomas J. Stanley* it was identified that more than GPA, IQ, college major, family opportunity, or business selection, one characteristic stood out. They were all doing something they loved. When you love what you are doing, chances are excellent you will succeed.

So many people complain about their work and many statistics that seem to support that it's the norm. Half of all respondents in a recent 2020 survey said they weren't satisfied with their jobs. Male suicides are highest on Sunday evenings when the weekend is over and the thought of returning to work is too much. For many people, work has become nothing more than a paycheck. It's become an accepted stance to hate our job and belittle the boss and company.

I have been blessed in this particular aspect of my life. I have never had to file for unemployment. My first job was 1975, and I retired in 2013. I had many jobs as an adolescent and young adult, mainly baling hay, mowing yards, and as a janitor's helper at the school I attended. I've read many articles that support part time work while going to school. Some students say they got better grades while they were working. They had to learn to use their time wisely and develop better study habits.

Much fuss is made about the minimum wage--It's too high or too low. Jim Rohn says this about minimum wage: "It's your starting point, it doesn't matter. It's not a bed you lie in your whole life, it's a ladder that you are expected to climb. Everyone has the same worth as a person, but it's our job to make ourselves more valuable to the marketplace. Then and only then will we earn more."

I heard of a study that was done that supports this. Graduating seniors were told to follow their hearts and not which job paid the most when selecting employers. After twenty years of working the group of 100 was asked two questions: *Did you chase the money or your passion?* Ninety-one admitted to chasing money. The other question, *have you attained a net worth of one million dollars?* None from the larger group had. Of the nine who admitted to following their heart, eight of the nine had attained net worth of over one million dollars. Many people would wonder how that can be. Think about it, if you enjoy your work, you'll be more pleasant to be around, you'll most likely be sought out for more opportunities that lead to advancement and promotion. Putting in more hours isn't a burden thus overtime opportunities and more pay.

In my working years the one constant I see as I look back was that I continued to learn. Continuous education kept me fresh and usually eager to go to work. I felt like I made a difference. Most days were filled with opportunities. I know it's not possible to feel this way 100% of the time, but you can be better. Your attitude will go a long way to your outlook. In the book *Twelve Pillars by Jim Rohn and Chris Widener* a statement is made over and over: *work harder on yourself than you do on your job.* I bought into this idea totally. By improving in as many aspects of your life as possible you'll influence others to do the same. It's not to say that there are no problems, but that all problems can be solved or at least made bearable. I've seen time and again that an employee is labeled a problem employee, only to find out if people are treated as you'd like to be treated, they'll perform. As a supervisor it's your responsibility to give feedback timely, good or bad. As an employee it's your responsibility to give 100% to the tasks assigned. When these actions happen, the sky's the limit to where the company as well as employees can go.

Some people are content with learning a job and keeping that for many years. There's nothing wrong with this way of thinking. However, I found I was easily bored with repetition. I enjoyed learning new things and challenging myself. When I look back at my career, I probably had nearly 40 jobs. This goes from part time jobs while in school to everything thereafter. That may seem like a lot but I found working in one area opened up other opportunities and adventure elsewhere. My last employment was at a company where I worked for over 30 years. However, while there I probably had over 25 different jobs / responsibilities that allowed me to stay fresh.

Looking back, I had a lot of great bosses--some not so great--but I learned from all of them. Even if it was just how *not* to do something. I kept learning and teaching. This is critical for your overall happiness and health because so many hours are spent at work. If you aren't passionate about your work, it will rub off and affect other aspects of your life.

A few lessons I learned along the way:

> Always give 100% and then some. When people see you can do quality, timely work, they'll most likely give you more opportunity. Some people think of this as being taken advantage of, but don't look at it that way. Do more than you are paid to do. In the long run it will pay off.
>
> Pay attention, ask questions, be diplomatic when doing. I always made changes in the way I did the job I was trained to do. Not because I thought I was smarter but because I found ways that made things more efficient.

I tried to get input upstream and downstream on how my job affected others. This may not apply as much to an assembly environment but most non-direct jobs have some flexibility. Whenever I trained someone, I explained, this is the way I do it, however if you find a better way please do so, advising your supervisor of the change and ensuring they concur.

Don't be afraid to look elsewhere. If you are in a large company many times better fits are around the corner. In some instances, you may have to quit. Just don't quit before you find work elsewhere. Being miserable helps no one. I've done retail, entrepreneur, manufacturing including laborer, inspection, and production control. Back to retail, then back to manufacturing where I started as a laborer, then staff, coordinator, and asst manager. From there I went to HR, then back to manufacturing, and then purchasing and finally engineering where I did a purchasing function.

In all those cases I always drew on experiences in past jobs and lessons learned in people interactions. More than once someone would say isn't your role _____? I never quit making suggestions even if they were outside my area of responsibility. Maybe it was their way of keeping some boundaries, but I've always felt if there is a better mousetrap, let's hear about it. Many times, the idea wasn't even something I had done, but something I saw that someone else had incorporated. I was simply letting others know about it, hoping it would make their lives better. Share your ideas and input for the good of your company.

On a Dan Miller podcast (48days.com) he explained that a doctor came to him for career coaching. The doctor explained he was miserable. He hated everything about being a doctor. Dan listened and asked more questions probing further. Eventually it was discovered he didn't hate every aspect.

He actually enjoyed feeling like he helped people. It was the insurance companies and paperwork that he despised.

Dan asked the doctor, what would you do if you could do anything you wanted? The doctor didn't hesitate, he replied, "Drive a truck!" It turned out the doctor became a doctor because his dad was as was his grandfather. They would be very disappointed if he left the profession. To make matters worse the doctor had become a drug user injecting himself with drugs and consequently ruining nearly all the veins in his body. He was currently shooting up on his feet when he came for help.

After listening to the doctor's story Dan suggested a plan. Rather than the doctor walking away from his education, what about employment in an emergency room on the weekend? There the doctor could patch people up, and therefore feel good about helping people, while also not having to mess with paperwork or insurance companies. In addition, many doctors don't care for weekend duty so he was able to make as much in two days of work that he normally did in five.

The even happier ending to the story was guess what the doctor does Monday through Friday? You guessed it, he drives a truck. And because his life is in balance and he doesn't despise his work, he has kicked his drug use.

Another of Dan's stories had to do with a preacher. He had a small congregation that couldn't support what he needed for his family so he was also a part time painter. When he approached Dan, he questioned how God could allow this to happen when he felt called to his work and yet wasn't able to fulfill his family responsibilities. Dan advised him that there was nothing noble in not being able to provide for his family. After much soul searching and prayer, the minister decided to leave preaching and focus on full time house painting. The most remarkable thing happened. His income greatly exceeded his past earnings, and his family life was much improved. In addition, he found he had a greater impact winning souls for Jesus as a painter than he felt he ever did as a preacher. The reason being, as a preacher your words are expected, whereas as a painter invariably you'll strike up a conversation with your customer and many times, religion is one. Being able to talk with people in their home while he worked for them had a greater impact than all the regulars he preached to on Sundays.

One last story I recall from Dan. A man he was coaching was dissatisfied with his work. Dan asked him, "If you could do anything you wanted and money wasn't an object what would you do?"

The man replied, "Read history books." He loved reading about history. Although it seems hard to imagine how a person could make money reading history books, that's exactly what he does now. As the market for teaching has changed with the expansion of homeschooling, this man now reads history books and records his enthusiastic voice to be replayed to eager students. There's a market for it, and he enjoys what he does while supporting his family.

My first job out of high school was at a local lumber yard. The lumber yard sold a variety of other goods as well, and I fixed windows and screens. Actually, I was hired to specifically fix windows and screens. They had a backlog of work, and it wasn't getting completed because it was no one in particular's job.

I was trained and spent the next two months doing nothing but repairing windows and screens. Sometimes when I called to advise the owner the screens were fixed, the customer forgot they'd ever brought one in for repair. The work was a bit simple and monotonous, but that allowed me to get pretty good at it.

Once that work was caught up I was trained to wait on customers, order inventory, stock shelves, load trucks and deliver products and more. It was very educational and I enjoyed that type of work because of the variety and learning so many new things. The only problem was It only paid minimum wage. Fortunately, my boss pulled me aside one day and told me he was going to bump my pay an extra twenty cents per hour. He said he thought I was doing good work and deserved it. I was on cloud nine for only a day; the following day he posted that the minimum wage was going up by the same amount.

Looking back, I think he should have told me that in the pep talk the day before. By not doing so I assumed his talk was just fluff and the only reason I got the raise was it was mandated.

Shortly thereafter I saw an ad in the local paper for a golf course manager. It seemed too good to be true. For a moment I told myself, *why apply, they'd never give a job like that to a 19-year-old.* Then I came to my senses and thought, *I'd never get the opportunity if I didn't try. The worst they could say was no and I'd be no worse off.*

I got an interview with a local businessman who had purchased the property as an investment. His goal was to break even on expenses while the land became worth more. He told me he had interviewed 34 people for the position but something told him I was the guy for the job. I was ecstatic.

The job was a nine-hole par three golf course and a driving range. I'd need to keep everything mowed and trimmed, fertilized, and watered. I'd be waiting on people, selling snacks and sandwiches, stocking the pop machine and more. All in all, I was an entrepreneur but didn't really know what that meant at that time. The reason I say I was an entrepreneur is that everything was my responsibility. If it failed it was on me, if it succeeded it was due to my efforts.

From March through October, it was seven days a week and sun up till sun down. Needless to say, I was busy. The operation didn't make enough money to hire a helper so I did 90% myself. Occasionally my younger brother would help mow if he could drive the tractor. Periodically my mom would run the shop allowing me to go out on a date or take a much-needed break, be it to play golf or softball.

As fall approached, I knew I'd need something for winter and had heard a local factory was hiring. I went for an interview and was hired within five minutes. The personnel manager wanted me to start right away. I told him I'd have to go back across town and get some work boots. He said no problem, I'll clock you in, just let me know when you're back.

I thought I must interview really well to sell him on myself in five minutes. Then reality hit me when I returned. The job was one of the most physical jobs I'd ever done. It was called the plater. There was a lot of lifting and a lot of walking. Had I not done a lot of hay baling in my younger years I would most likely have been intimidated.

Many people started after I did and many would last two hours. At first break they'd disappear never to be seen again. I don't know the actual numbers but I'd guess half of the people who started there were gone in a month.

After ninety days workers were allowed to bid on other openings in the factory. When my ninety days were up I started looking. Shortly after that an inspection job was posted. It sounded interesting and I applied. After a series of interviews, I was selected.

Some of the guys I worked with gave me a hard time once they heard I was leaving. Some said *that's a second shift job, you'll be there forever.* To which I replied *we're on second shift now, what's the difference?* The way they saw it was due to turnover on the plater, they'd get off second shift long before me.

I started my new job training on the first shift. The guy who trained me was older with a lot of experience. We worked together at least four weeks before plans were to place me on the second shift. However, before everything was finalized my trainer had a heart attack. The third shift inspector had seniority so he came for days. The second shift inspector didn't want a third shift job so I was placed there. What better a place for a 19-year-old?

By now it was approaching spring. I enjoyed the inspection work. I was learning new things using micrometers and calipers. I was learning to read blueprints and parts of the manufacturing process. The people I worked with were good to be around and working third shift gave me evenings open. It was the next best thing to working days.

I knew I was going back to the golf course because that's the job I really enjoyed. But now that I'd secured a good job for the winter months, I was hesitant to give it up. I wondered, could I do both? I reasoned I could. *I'm young, I* told myself. If my brother would take on a little more, I was sure I could swing it.

From March-April I was working 7:00am to 9:00pm at the golf course and 11:00pm to 7:00am at the factory. That left two hours to sleep. I squeezed in a couple more hours in between waiting on customers but my summers were a blur. What made matters worse, the factory's busiest time was in the summer. So, there were many six-day workweeks and some seven-day workweeks. I remember praying for rain.

My mom would periodically run the golf shop concession for me when she could tell I was running low on energy. However, I maintained this pace for three years total. It wasn't easy committing to a golf league or playing softball tournaments, let alone dating, but I did.

At one point the owner offered to sell me the property. I recall saying *what bank would give a twenty-year-old a loan for over $100,000?* To which he replied *we don't need a bank, let's just do a handshake.*

I really wanted to go through with buying the property, but looking at the numbers scared me. It seemed like I'd run the golf course and all proceeds would go towards the payment. Then it would take the factory job to pay for everything else. I didn't think I could do that for twenty more years.

Looking back, it wouldn't have been easy, but I could have done it. One thing I never considered was my payment was fixed while my income opportunity was variable and on the rise. If I had raised the fees to play over time, while increasing play I probably could have afforded his offer. Furthermore, as the ground appreciated, I could have sold it for a nice profit.

I was too conservative and lacked the knowledge I needed to make the best decision. However, missing an opportunity there didn't slow me down in my quest to do my best. I applied for another in-house position at the factory and got it. This time in Production Control working first shift. The job was a small pay increase and was salary, as opposed to hourly. Because it was new, it was exciting. Customers would place orders and my job was to get them through the shop on time.

I had a board with all open orders listed. I sorted them by due dates. There were probably 1500 orders at any one time with quantities ranging from 1,000 to 1,000,000 pieces. The person who trained me showed me everything he knew and turned me loose.

I began by learning about all the people I'd be working with. Primarily it was management of various departments; everyone from the buyers of steel to the foreman in departments that stamped the pieces, and finished them, and processes in between.

I got to know several of the hourly workers as well, already having known some of them through my outside hobbies. One man in particular took me aside and gave me intense training on how my job affected him. He was a tooling coordinator.

There was information I had access to that was meaningless to me but meant everything to him. Once he explained to me that if we could run jobs sequenced by these tooling numbers we could increase efficiency, a light bulb went off in my head.

I went back to my desk and resorted the orders by these newly understood tooling numbers. I then needed a way to make the due dates stand out so I started a color-coded sequence. In addition, I worked with a computer programmer explaining that I got seven different reports that had redundant information on them. I further explained if we could make one report that had all this data on one page, we could save thousands of pages per month.

We worked off and on for months on this project. He was excited as was I to be doing something that we could see was going to be monumental in increasing our efficiency while saving paper and money. We still had to do things the old way while we were perfecting this new method.

Eventually it was done. One report taking the place of seven as well as an order board that was sorted by tooling sequence and color coded by due dates. I could now do my job in twenty hours whereas when I began, I was spending 45-60 hours.

Efficiency flourished and overdue orders became a thing of the past. However, at this time I was not feeling as attached to my work, because I couldn't see where we would go next. My boss was fairly young, as was his. It seemed like I might be stuck. What was exciting had come to an end. I knew I needed more and, as fate would have it, an opening at another lumber yard appeared. I interviewed and was offered a job.

I approached my boss and explained I had a job offer. I asked if he could come up with a raise. He said there was nothing available and his hands were tied. I then gave my two weeks' notice.

Two weeks passed, and I trained my replacement. On my last day my boss told me he was able to come up with a nice raise. I declined. I was humiliated to say the least. Waiting until the last minute like that?! He even brought up the fact that because my wife was pregnant, the new company would not pay for those medical costs. I told him I realized that but the time was right for a move.

Going to this new job was easy in that so much of what I had learned five years earlier was all coming back. Being this was a larger operation, there were new things to learn, but I had the basics covered. The people I worked with were great. I was an indoor salesman working with two experienced other salesmen.

I worked in this position for a couple of years. The pay matched the factory position and, with bonuses based on sales, actually exceeded. However, within a year of starting, a recession hit and the bonuses dried up. With my income decreasing I needed more dollars to support my family. Honda had recently added a factory in the area. It was time to see if it was for me.

I applied and was called in for an interview. The process was subsequent interviews once you passed the first. Eventually I made it through the hiring process and began another chapter in my employment career. I was placed in the weld department with ten other associates. At that time the auto plant had recently started, and we were making 40 cars per day.

I worked two years as an entry level employee. During that time, we were ramping up production to 300 vehicles per shift. Every other week we brought in more associates to assist with more production. We were constantly breaking down jobs we'd done into smaller increments so that each new employee had a piece to do. In time the job I hired into while producing 40 cars per day was done by eight people when we hit 300 per day.

There was a lot of daily overtime during that ramp up. Production needed to be met and breakdowns in equipment met an hour overtime regularly. In addition, we worked a lot of Saturdays to do projects that would increase our efficiency through the week.

Eventually it was decided that we needed some off-line staff to do jobs that required overtime to do. The department set up some interviews to select two associates for quality and another two associates for the planning group. I applied and received one of the planning group positions.

I was excited to venture into a new position and the ability to learn new skills. However, my excitement was short-lived. We were little more than an absenteeism coverage pool, meaning as associates would not come to work, supervisors would pluck us from our new position to fill in for them for the day. In some ways it was worse than working the line daily, because we never knew what job we'd be doing and with little training. All the while being expected to carry out our new task working over time.

In time everything worked out, but those first six months I wondered if this new assignment was worth the bother. Periodically we would be asked to support which was our culture. We knew we'd not be a viable company if we didn't meet daily production numbers. But 80% of the time we were working on our new assignments.

Those assignments were mainly in preparing for new technology, or efficiency improvements and new model activities. We'd plan the work through the week and line up everything needed but most of our activity would be off hours, primarily weekends. What we could do ourselves we would, when we needed additional support, we'd quote out contractors and work together.

In time the company announced an expansion that would double our production. My job was modified to work on that team to make that happen. It was everything from demolishing the original line, sending equipment to Mexico and other

U.S. plants to actually taking up concrete that wasn't four years old and digging new pits to hold the new equipment.

There were hundreds of people to work with from all aspects of the trades. We worked hand in hand to ensure the work was to print checking and double checking. An additional task I picked up was working with production control to track and expedite the equipment coming from Japan.

This was an interesting time and very busy. Thousands of crates were headed to the United States and, working with the Japanese, we developed a sequence of what needed to be opened first so that we could assemble the items. We could route items through the Panama Canal up to the port of Baltimore in four weeks as the least costly option. The other option was usually West Coast like Portland then truck the items, saving two weeks.

There were permits that needed to be obtained because much of the equipment was oversize. Sometimes needing escorts thus driving up the costs.

In time the line was up and running and I was given one last assignment. I had to go through all the packing lists of equipment and, working with production control and our legal department, make a list of what we had received. We were going to be charged tariffs based on classifications of equipment. For example, a weld machine had a two percent tariff where an electrical component had a six percent tariff. This was adding up to tens of millions of dollars.

Our argument with customs was that the electrical controllers along with other pieces should be considered weld equipment because that's the only function they had. The whole process was painstaking and took around four months. In the end the courts agreed and we saved millions of dollars on the project but also set the precedent for millions of dollars to be saved in future.

Once this project was complete, I was assigned to working with maintenance and tasked with setting up a spare parts cage. We had thousands of parts without much organization. It was important that as a machine broke down that we had the part and knew where it was.

In time this grew to creating a cage of maintenance parts as well as consumables items like gloves, sealer, and items used in everyday production. This was viewed as money wasted by some concerning the staffing that was required. However, running out of product because someone didn't take the time to document what was taken, thus not reordered, was soon determined to be money well spent rather than a waste.

My boss moved on to a new position and I took his role while maintaining my supervisory roles in my current position. Here I added responsibilities in production control, safety, training, improvement programs, and manpower control including HR issues like promotions, evaluations, hiring and disciplinary issues. In addition, monitoring attendance and sick leave as well as temporary positions for abnormal issues.

Earlier I'd been exposed to production control through my time working with our expansion. Then I became familiar with purchasing and accounting working with the maintenance and consumable parts. Now I was working with Human Resources on people issues. I'd become more recognizable outside my department than inside.

I worked another three years with this group improving the way we did things. My time was primarily spent on the manpower issues but I dabbled in all the other areas mentioned as well. There were multiple people tasked with the oversight of the items mentioned earlier and I was their supervisor.

HR asked me if I'd ever consider making a move to their department and after considering it I thought it might be time for a change. I doubted anything would ever happen that our company would close but learning what goes on in HR could be a nice career enhancement. After all, most businesses have HR departments. In my thinking, I would be learning some new skills and making myself more marketable at the same time.

After working in HR for two years a manufacturing department was having problems and I was asked if I would be willing to assist. My time in HR was an education but I was ready for a change. I took on the new responsibility and along with a couple other new management members we were able to turn things around. The department went from the bottleneck of the plant to running like a well-oiled machine.

My responsibilities were almost identical to those I had prior to HR and while it was exciting at first because of the different plant and different people the work soon became familiar. Then a new opportunity presented itself in the purchasing department.

In the beginning I was assigned as a capital equipment and construction buyer. I had been in many of these negotiations from the department side but now was the official buyer legally. Again, I learned a lot and was exposed to many things I never knew or was exposed to especially from the legal standpoint.

Next, I was in a role as a commodity leader where I purchased items for the plant and negotiated contracts. Eventually I was put in charge of several buyers and worked with them on strategies and planning.

From there I was assigned special projects for the group and came up with some creative ways to honor suppliers who were achieving and exceeding expectations while at the same time encouraging those who weren't to perform better.

One of my managers I worked with had moved to our engineering group and eventually asked me to rejoin him at yet another plant. Although I was happy where I was and still felt there was more to accomplish, I agreed to make another change.

My last seven years was working with engineers to find local suppliers to assist in our needs and lessen our dependence on Japan. It was a gratifying experience to meet several new people and work together with the current buyers and assist in any way needed.

There's a lot of information I've included about my career that most likely won't mean anything to most people who read it. However, my reasoning for including it is for you to see how much variety is available if you desire. I know people who got a job and worked the same basic job their whole life. I'm not saying that's not good, but for me I enjoyed variety and learning new things. I think it probably stunted my upward growth in the company but for me I felt I was fairly compensated and new adventures were more important than more money and dealing with the same issues.

You need to decide for yourself what career path you'll choose. In the book 48Days to the Work you Love by Dan Miller he explains 80% of college graduates are working in a field totally unrelated to their college major within ten years of graduation. Additionally, he adds that in ten years 90% of what an engineer is taught in college will be available on a computer and 50 % of what an electronics student learns as a freshman is obsolete by their senior year.

Speaking from experience I recall a young engineer confiding in me after being hired that he had a decision to make. He had a degree in weld engineering and he felt his job responsibilities had little to no need for what he'd learned in school. He was contemplating quitting although he made good money with nice benefits because he felt he was throwing his four-year education away. After much soul searching, he did stay with the company, and rose many levels in management despite never feeling like his college years were advantageous to his career.

A company I worked with was having turnover problems. It was a machine shop and it was doing quite well but found many people would come there for a dollar more on the hour than they were currently getting. However, within a year they'd find someone else who was paying yet another dollar more. Consequently, all that time spent training them on the operation was gone. The owner realized that the employees who were the most loyal came from the small town they resided in. That gave him an idea. He approached the local school principal and asked for five boys that were good kids but most likely weren't going to college. He had the five meet him the following Monday.

He told them he'd like to keep the shop clean and gave each a broom. He also asked them to assist the workers with small tasks if asked, like lifting parts baskets off the floor or moving products. They were paid for two hours after school each day and five hours on Saturdays.

The plan worked. By Saturday three of the boys had quit. They were either bored, or felt the work was beneath them. The owner then pulled the remaining two workers into his office. He explained he had an opportunity to run by them. He said running his machines required some technical skills that he was sure they could learn but felt their learning would be accelerated if they attended the local technical college for a two-year degree.

He further explained, "If you'll agree to this, I'll pay 100% of your schooling. In addition, if you come here on Saturdays, I'll double your cleaning wages to assist in the shop and learn some hands-on skills. I guarantee you, if you follow through on this, you'll graduate in two years and walk into a job that pays $80,000 per year right out of school with no debt."

They both jumped at the chance. With overtime their salaries are actually closer to $100,000. In addition, the owner has repeated the process each year for the past five years. Locals have a great job to start with and tend to stay because of the pay and benefits. As they start families, they are even more committed to staying in the area because of extended families such as parents and grandparents.

I've interviewed many people (thousands) in my work years. I was surprised how many lacked what seems like common sense interview etiquette. Things like, maintaining eye contact, being on time, being attentive, asking some well thought of follow up questions, (not necessarily money related) and closing with a firm handshake and a thank you.

Basic mistakes people make:

1) Lack of gratitude for their work
2) Doing less than they are capable of
3) Complaining / whining
4) Not looking elsewhere if they are miserable, comfortable misery
5) Talking about management rather than making a suggestion for improvement

Questions to consider: On a scale of 1 – 10 with 10 being perfection how would you rate yourself in this area? ____

Consider:

1) Do I enjoy my work?
2) I am regularly excited to get back to work after the weekend or vacation?
3) Do I feel valued and or appreciated at work?
4) When getting a performance evaluation does it seem to be a fair assessment?
5) Do my opinions count, are they constructive?

Takeaway:

- The single best expert on finding work you love is Dan Miller His website is 48days.com He is a genius on this subject and 80% of his material is free. He has a blog, a weekly newsletter, and a weekly podcast I listen to religiously. He shares so many stories of people not a good fit at their work and how they overcame it. If you take nothing else but this, subscribe to his newsletter and listen to his podcast. Additionally, he has a book "48 days to the work and life you love" just released a 20th anniversary edition.
- If you're in a job you hate, make plans to move on. First, though, take the time to know what you're looking for, and don't quit your current work until you are hired.
- Sometimes the problem might lie within, look honestly.
- Think of the things you are grateful for in a job. Suppose you lost your job, then looked for months and found nothing. You'd most likely welcome your previous job back.
- Finally, I've read once a person is hired their opportunities for promotions are 85% of the time based on skills that aren't technical. These skills include interpersonal skills like communication, attitude, enthusiasm, and self-discipline. If you have personal skills, you'll eventually be found. In the meantime, keep improving.

CHAPTER 6

FINANCE

Never trade what you want most for what you want now.

What is it?

Personal finance is your money and your assets. Many people's view on personal finance is completely wrong, but they fall in love with the idea and dig a large hole before they know what hit them. So many people think they need or deserve things. This leads to debt, overpaying for almost anything, and habits that are hard to break.

It's been said that financial problems wreck more marriages than any other reason. Financial issues can wreak havoc on any and all other aspects of our lives as well. When we overspend or simply spend for the sake of spending, we often don't have what we need to make ends meet. The pain this causes can ruin marriages, relationships, health, careers, and self-esteem.

There are a few key principles that can make all the difference. They are simple to acquire but not easy to maintain. However, if you are able stick to a plan, you might be able to live tomorrow like others only dream of.

My experience

Finance is an area that always came easy for me. Easy, as far as understanding, not necessarily as feeling I ever had enough. My dad instilled many traits that I adopted at an early age that I believe made a big impact. One of the biggest ideas that stuck with me was:

There's a difference between wants and needs. You may think you need something but if you can wait a day, things will probably look different tomorrow.

Dad never had a credit card until he was in his 60's and that was to get mail order medicine without the hassle of ordering and paying with a check before receiving. His motto was *If I don't have cash, I can't afford it.* That went for everything but the house.

He also made good use of everything, salvaging used lumber, nuts, bolts and even bent nails. I recall questioning him about the bent nails, suggesting his time was worth more than the money saved. He was quick to add however; it depends on what you do with that time.

I recall him discussing with my older brother the need to save. I was five years younger and listened intently although trying not to look like I was eavesdropping. Dad made a point that my brother could live in our home after graduation rent free if he'd save a large portion of his check. Otherwise, he'd expect rent that was about the same that was expected to be saved. My brother said he didn't want to be told how much to save so he'd pay the rent.

My interpretation might not be 100% correct but I thought, why not put the money in the bank where it's yours, rather than give it away as rent. At any rate that sticks out in my mind and as a result I became a saver, probably almost to a fault.

I had many jobs growing up. Mowing yards around the age of 12, then moving to farm work and baling hay for several years. Around the age of 16 I got the opportunity to work at our school where we did painting, waxing floors, and general work to get the building ready for the new school year. Once school started, I was given three hours after school to clean it. I missed some of the outdoor aspects of farm work but this job was easier and it was year-round. That in itself made it worth it.

Even with these minimum wage jobs I was able to save large portions of my earnings and save for my first car. Once I started dating, I had to keep out more money for movies and dinner but everything else was saved.

I started thinking about retirement when I was 18. I had a grandpa that worked until he was 65 and on his last day of work, he picked up his check and gold watch and proceeded to have a heart attack on the way home. He died that same day.

I suppose that I could have viewed my grandpa's untimely death in one of two ways. The first being, life is short, we don't know how long we have to live so eat, drink and be merry. The second way to perceive that event, however, could be that it's sad a person could work his whole life and then not live to enjoy the fruits of his labor. Therefore, I will work hard and save my money allowing me to retire at an earlier age.

My dad worked for a company that had a 30 year and out opportunity. My younger brother was still in school so dad stayed until he graduated, but he still got out at 51 years old. He developed cancer at 62 and passed away at 67. However, I was always grateful that he had over eleven years of good health that he and mom were able to enjoy with friends and family.

Saving / planning

I realize that none of our days are guaranteed, and we could go tomorrow, but that mindset should never be the cause of failing to plan for our future. There are many reasons people give for not starting early to save for retirement, but it's a habit that has many benefits that I can attest to.

Following is an example of the value in starting to save early. In the left column the person began saving as a 25-year-old. Saving until age 35 and stopping. Overall savings, $55,000. The person in the right column didn't start saving until age 35 but contributed $5,000 per year until age 60. Overall, they saved $130,000.

Despite the person who saved only $55,000, their total at age 60 with an 8% return is $615,580.

The person who saved $130,000 by age 60 only has $431,754. They saved $75,000 more but have $183,826 less because they started later in life to save. In addition, they'll never catch up.

age		.08 return		age		.08 return	
25	$5,000	$400	$5,400	25			
26	$5,000	$832	$11,232	26			
27	$5,000	$1,299	$17,531	27			
28	$5,000	$1,802	$24,333	28			
29	$5,000	$2,347	$31,680	29			
30	$5,000	$2,934	$39,614	30			
31	$5,000	$3,569	$48,183	31			
32	$5,000	$4,255	$57,438	32			
33	$5,000	$4,995	$67,433	33			
34	$5,000	$5,795	$78,227	34			
35	$5,000	$6,658	$89,886	35	$5,000	$400	$5,400
36		$7,191	$97,076	36	$5,000	$832	$11,232
37		$7,766	$104,843	37	$5,000	$1,299	$17,531
38		$8,387	$113,230	38	$5,000	$1,802	$24,333
39		$9,058	$122,288	39	$5,000	$2,347	$31,680
40		$9,783	$132,071	40	$5,000	$2,934	$39,614
41		$10,566	$142,637	41	$5,000	$3,569	$48,183
42		$11,411	$154,048	42	$5,000	$4,255	$57,438
43		$12,324	$166,372	43	$5,000	$4,995	$67,433
44		$13,310	$179,682	44	$5,000	$5,795	$78,227
45		$14,375	$194,056	45	$5,000	$6,658	$89,886
46		$15,525	$209,581	46	$5,000	$7,591	$102,476
47		$16,766	$226,347	47	$5,000	$8,598	$116,075
48		$18,108	$244,455	48	$5,000	$9,686	$130,761
49		$19,556	$264,012	49	$5,000	$10,861	$146,621
50		$21,121	$285,132	50	$5,000	$12,130	$163,751
51		$22,811	$307,943	51	$5,000	$13,500	$182,251
52		$24,635	$332,578	52	$5,000	$14,980	$202,231
53		$26,606	$359,185	53	$5,000	$16,579	$223,810
54		$28,735	$387,920	54	$5,000	$18,305	$247,115
55		$31,034	$418,953	55	$5,000	$20,169	$272,284
56		$33,516	$452,469	56	$5,000	$22,183	$299,466
57		$36,198	$488,667	57	$5,000	$24,357	$328,824
58		$39,093	$527,760	58	$5,000	$26,706	$360,530
59		$42,221	$569,981	59	$5,000	$29,242	$394,772
60		$45,598	$615,580	60	$5,000	$31,982	$431,754

Some stats

As mentioned, personal finance is one of the leading causes of divorce. Additionally, 70% of Americans live paycheck to paycheck. 97% carry credit card debt, meaning they don't pay off credit balances monthly. Depending on your view of money it can either run you or you manage it.

Further statistics show:

FINANCE

Less than 4% of workers think they'll be able to retire by age 55.
36% of workers have not yet begun to save anything.
44% have less than $500 in savings.
60% have less than $25,000.
29% of people age 65 and up still make a mortgage payment.
27% of people age 65 have credit card debt.

Social security was intended to supplement retirement, however 22% of married couples and 47% of single people on Social Security depend almost entirely on that income.

I once heard if all the money in the world were evenly distributed amongst the entire population, in a short time it would be back in the hands of those who had it in the first place. That's why so many athletes or lottery winners are broke, because they never learned how to use money.

The message I have gained and lived on from experience and learning is this: Your income has to exceed your spending.

Make it a game

One exercise I like to do every year is assess my net worth. Remember your financial net worth has nothing to do with your worth as a spouse, parent, worker, or human being. It's simply your financial health at a snapshot in time. January 1st is a great day to do this exercise. Simply take the value of everything you own and subtract all you owe. The balance is net worth as of that date in time. The goal is to watch that grow. This would include investments, 401k, house, cars, etc.

Brushing your teeth, eating a balanced diet, and exercising regularly are good habits. Likewise spending less than you earn and saving for a rainy day are the equivalents of those habits in the financial world.

Satisfaction isn't so much of getting what you want as wanting what you have. There are two ways to be rich; one is to have great wealth; the other is to have few wants. You need to find ways to make the most of the money that does pass through your hands, and to never lose sight of everything that is far more important than money.

Having the desire to assist your children with future educational needs is a normal want. However, doing so before your own goals are achieved may be a financial mistake. The college financial aid system penalizes you for savings outside your retirement accounts and penalizes you even more if the money is invested in the child's name.

Don't let the spending habits of others dictate yours. In addition, don't go shopping thinking buying something will make you happy. If it does, it's only for a short time. Once you get the bill, you'll realize you've fallen victim to emotional spending. My daughter-in-law told me that she likes to go "window shopping" online. She will fill a virtual shopping cart with things, she'll even add coupons to see how much she can save, and then she closes it down and walks away. She says that it's enough to get the "high" of shopping, but then she doesn't have the junk she never really needed or the money spent. Do something else, you'll thank yourself when these habits give you a lifestyle that others dream about.

Dave Ramsey is probably the most well-known financial guru and in reading his seven-step plan I'd have to say I agree with 90-95% of his advice. The only two areas that are different for me are credit card use, and if you have debt, how you go about paying it off. However, he does say, conventional wisdom did not put you in this predicament, so conventional wisdom won't get you out. With that statement I'd agree 100%.

Dave's 7 step plan:

1) Save $1,000 fast: emergency fund for car repair, home repairs etc.
2) Debt snowball: pay down / payoff debt by listing your debts smallest to largest, attack the smallest with a vengeance, then move down the list until debt free
3) Save 3-6 months' income
4) Maximize retirement savings
5) College support
6) Payoff the mortgage
7) Build wealth (live life – have fun – help others)

To be debt free and have money in the bank is a great feeling. The key is to live on less than you make. Be mature about your choices. Ben Franklin was famous for his line, "A penny saved is a penny earned." The Bible tells us man cannot serve two masters, and the borrower is a servant to the lender.

The idea of living beneath your means has always made sense to me. You can pay me now or pay me later was a phrase from a commercial I recall. As I mentioned earlier my dad taught me lessons on this regularly without saying a word. He'd tackle any fix-it job around the house, farm, or car. He wouldn't buy anything until he had cash to pay for it and reuse anything, including bent nails. We didn't take many vacations growing up but did enjoy life experiences.

Many people go through life living paycheck to paycheck, and I imagine that's a hole that's hard to dig yourself out of, yet I know it's possible. Although I mentioned this area of life has been a strength for me, I've still listened to Dave Ramsey's advice, listening to carefully, in the event I've missed anything. There's always something to learn, so keep your eyes open and listen carefully.

Make it a game part 2

My family just recently cut our land line. Many people started doing that five-ten years ago. The only calls we were getting were telemarketers. We cut our cable about five years ago. So many times my wife and I would look at each other and say *we're paying $80 a month for this selection?!* It's not that we can't afford these things, rather why pay for something that has little value? Free antenna TV is just fine. We've since splurged on Hulu.

My wife and I use credit cards a lot, and although this goes against Dave Ramsey advice, it's worked well for us. If you aren't disciplined, however, I advise against it. Research shows that people buy 37% more with a credit card than they would with cash. The theory is there is no "pain" associated with a credit card, whereas when you hand over cash there is the sense of how hard you had to work for that.

I think McDonalds was the first to put in credit card machines for fast food purchases. At one time most would have thought it was ridiculous to pay for fast food this way but now it's the norm. I heard a business owner tell me that 90% of her customers pay with a credit card.

The key is to pay off the balance every month. In searching for data on this I got various figures so rather than list any numbers my advice is to **never** carry a balance. I've heard that this one practice will put you in the top 5% of people in America. Meaning that 95% of Americans carry a balance.

As I mentioned earlier the key is discipline. Don't buy things just because you can. Buy them because you need them. Additionally, I have my credit card set up to automatically deduct from my savings or money market account the total balance due so that I have no interest payment. Remember 95% of Americans don't do this. I did. I retired at age 56 whereas 96% of Americans can't do that, do you see the correlation?

Most credit cards offer some sort of incentive to use their card. Mine offers $100 cash for every $11,500 spent on their card. If you have the discipline to use as I've mentioned make sure you sign up and take advantage of the offer. On average I get back $300-400 per year. That's money you are throwing away if you don't take advantage of the offers that come with a credit card.

Budget

Make sure you know where your money is going. Many people advocate making a budget and sticking to it. Depending on where you are in your knowledge of finance this can make 100% sense or it could be overkill. However, if you've never made a budget, I highly suggest you do it. Research where your money goes, every dollar, every month. This will take some time the first time you do it.

I'm including a spreadsheet to help you get started if needed.

Yearly Household Budget			
Housing		**Entertainment**	
Mortgage / Rent		Vacation	
Phone		Hobby	
Cable		Pets	
Electric		Magazine / Books	
Gas /heat		Multimedia	
Water / trash		Restaurants	
Maintenance		Movies, Concerts, etc	
Property Tax			
Sub total		Sub total	

The 8 Facets of Life

Transportation	
Gas	
Maintenance	
Tolls	
License / taxes	
Public Transportation	
Sub total	

Personal	
Food	
Gifts	
Clothes	
Shoes	
Dry Cleaning	
Hair / Makeup	
Health club	
Other	
Sub total	

Taxes	
Federal	
State	
Local	
Social Security	
Medicare	
Sub total	

Health Care	
Copay's	
Drugs	
Sub total	

Debt	
Credit Card	
Car loan / payment	
Student Loan	
Personal Loans	
Sub total	

Insurance	
Car	
Home	
Disability	
Life	
Health	
Sub total	

Children			**Charity**	
Daycare			Donations	
Babysitter			other	
Toys				
Clothes			Sub total	
Other				
Sub total			**Grand total**	

I'm also including some recommendations for % of money to be used for each category. I used several sources as well as my own experience to compile the following guidelines. Remember though they are recommendations. If your income is very high or very low the percentages will vary.

As an example, if your income is low the necessities will be high whereas with a higher income, they would be much lower, but your savings should be much higher.

> Charity 10-15%
> Savings 5-10%
> Housing 25-35%
> Utilities 5-10%
> Food 5-15%
> Transportation 10-15%
> Clothing 2-7%
> Medical 5-10%
> Personal 5-10%
> Recreation 5-10%
> Debts 5-10%

Remember your percentage can only add up to 100 so you can't use the high end on all of the recommendations. If you use a smaller number in one area that will allow you to spend more in another area. The key is to live within your income and hopefully below.

If you have areas that seem out of balance don't panic. Just decide if that's ok. Someone might have a higher house payment than is recommended. However, if you are satisfied in not taking yearly vacations because this is your dream home and the money saved will offset the house payment then that's ok.

The same goes for any other area. If money is needed in one area you will have to decide where it's going to come from. It's either reallocated or you need to make more money, such as getting a second job, having a yard sale, or seeking a promotion.

Planning

When you set your budget, this is an opportunity for husband, wife and even children to come together and discuss what's really important. The discussion might go something like this: we haven't been able to save enough for our planned Disney vacation this year. If we were to still go, we'll need to forgo our new school clothes plan by 50%. In addition, we had planned on upgrading our van this year, that will need to be put off another year. We could cut cable and cell phones and be able to pull it off. Or we could postpone the vacation another year and do something locally with the money we've saved.

Remember people will support what they help create. This goes for children as well. Think of the learning experience this would help the kids with as well. Learning that life is a compromise as a 16-year-old will no doubt come in handy as an adult, be it with money handling or relationships and more.

Once you've made a budget and have a good idea where your money is going it's best to share that if possible. I realize some people won't care or say they don't understand that kind of talk, but if your spouse is on the same page with your finances this can make life so much more enjoyable. There will be things you can't agree on, hopefully money won't be one of them. In the event you and your spouse went through the budgeting process together then you've already got a leg up on most couples.

Even after you have a handle on your finances there are still things that can be done. One thing I'd suggest is to set your bills up on auto pay. You can't haggle with your electric provider for instance. They probably have a small discount if the bill is paid by a certain date. Set up an autopay so you'll never miss the discount. You'll still receive a bill showing usage so if you feel there is an issue you can speak with them. The same can be done for most other expenses.

Some of my bills allow a credit card to be used with no excess charge. If that's an option that's my first choice. As I mentioned earlier my credit card is paid off regularly so there's no need to set up another payment method and I'm getting some earnings although they are modest. If they don't allow that or charge a fee, I use a direct payment method through my checking account. Any bank or credit union can help you set that up.

Make it a game

Another recommendation is to comparison shop to be sure you're getting a fair deal. Notice I didn't say the best deal but a fair deal. As an example, I'd been doing business with a particular insurance company and had no concerns. I'd competitively shopped periodically and usually found the savings to be minimal like $30 per year. Having a relationship in place that didn't warrant to me the need to change.

Homeowners make a claim on average of once per seventeen years. I got to thinking and realized that was me as well. I then comparison shopped using higher deductibles and found around $200 savings. That caught my eye. If you do that always make sure you are comparing apples to apples. As far as the relationship, that is something you'll have to decide if it's worth continuing. In my case I told my agent I'd put this off for years but felt the savings couldn't be overlooked. We shook hands and moved on.

Cars are the biggest expense, aside from your home, where people can save money. Usually buying new cars can't be justified. We hear how the minute you drive it off the lot it has lost value. Everyone needs dependable transportation. I'm not saying you don't. It's Just that a two-year-old car or more is probably the best economic decision because of the immediate depreciation a car has from the time you take it off the lot. If you tried to sell a car a week or month after you bought it no one would pay you near what you paid for it. They'd just go to the dealer to get the extras like free oil changes and car washes etc. If you paid $20,000 for a new vehicle it would depreciate $4000 to 6000 in the first year. As a rule of thumb in 5 years a vehicle can lose 60% or more of their value. (nerdwallet.com)

Even if you aren't handy the price of maintenance isn't that bad if you look around.

The biggest area where most of us could save even more money is dining out. I know my eating habits have changed over time, and it seems that most of society spends a good deal of their money on dining out. There are ways to do this economically. I know people who refuse to eat at fast food restaurants, be it they think the food isn't nutritious, or it's beneath them, I'm not sure. But my wife and I enjoy eating fast food periodically and feel it's a value. There are many other ways to save money too, including Groupon offers to local restaurants, coupons or fundraisers, "Dash Passes", Kids Eat Free nights, etc.

One of my favorite restaurants is Texas Roadhouse. At one time I always ordered filet when dining there. I justified the extra price saying, we only dine here once every couple months so this is my indulgence. When my sons went off to college, they both worked at Texas Roadhouse. One of them told me that I ought to try the sirloin. It's the piece right next to the filet and tastes pretty good at half the price. The next time I went I did just that. It tasted great, and I've been enjoying that cut of steak ever since, at half the price I used to pay.

Justification

The fact is we'll justify whatever we want, be it high-priced menu items, or expensive vacations. Years ago, we did an expensive Disney vacation, and it easily cost a month's salary. The vacation was something I saved an entire year to afford. Life is made up of experiences, and I didn't want to short change my children. That was my justification. I know some families who do these kinds of vacations yearly. I've always bought into the fact that happiness is not in things or events, but in experiences with family and friends. You can argue that is exactly what an expensive vacation brings. However, if you can't pay cash, my belief is you can't afford it. And the joy you get from the experience is short lived when the cost of paying for it is doubled when you make payments with all the interest charged. My point is, know where your money is going and determine if you are getting the value you deserve. You work too hard for your money to be taken advantage of.

How much is enough

I once heard a radio talk show host ask callers to call in and share two things: 1) how much money they are currently making and 2) how much money would it take to live comfortably? One of the first callers said he was making $25,000 per year but if he could make $50,000, he'd be set. Someone later that made $50,000 thought they'd need $90-100,000. On and on it went. Everyone thought if they could double their existing income their troubles would go away.

Yet I'm sure we've all heard of an elderly person passing away, living like a pauper their whole life and leaving millions to a charity. An interesting story I once heard was a preacher who was visiting a widow in a run-down cabin, dirt floor, no running water. He asked her what she'd do if she came into a lot of money. She thought for a bit and said I suppose I'd give it to the poor. Never seeing any need for anything herself.

I think that's the key--don't fall victim to the "keeping up with the Joneses". Happiness is different for everyone but money isn't the answer. I had a brother pass away at an early age and the pastor asked me if I'd like to speak. Initially I said no but later changed my mind. In looking at the crowd I recall a thought that came to me and has stuck ever since. Seeing all those people make the time to attend on a weekday, using their vacation time, made me realize, wealth has nothing to do with money!

Investments

Buy quality stocks and or mutual funds. Slow and steady makes sense although not as fun as buying a stock that makes a 300% return. The trouble is finding that without losing a lot before you do. If you desire to look for the high yield potential, do it without jeopardizing your nest egg.

I've watched stocks for years and wished I would have pulled the trigger on a few purchases. When Apple stock was selling in the one dollar range a friend of mine said Steve Jobs was being hired back and it seemed like a good time to buy. The stock held the one to two-dollar range for around six years then exploded to the $175 range.

The same thing happened with Ford around 2008-2009. Their stock dropped to around a dollar and within a year was over $15 per share. McDonalds has had steady slow growth from the 1970's to around 2005 then exploded from around $30 per share to over $160 per share.

There are many more examples I could share but the point is you don't have to buy penny stock of companies that may very well go broke to hit a homerun. You could just find a company that's either down for the time being or recently found a niche that could bring in some nice returns.

If you enjoy watching the market and studying businesses that's great. My advice would be to do your own research or work with a reputable firm. Don't get your data from the media or Uncle Joe. In the late 1990's I was tasked with finding an investment company for our church. A group of us interviewed three companies and settled on Edward D. Jones. The company generally gets high marks from its customers as well as financial watchdog groups. However, you must trust the individual completely too.

Shortly after closing that deal for our church, I also entered into an agreement as a personal customer. I think their fees are a little higher than some but again I'm looking for the trust issue as worth enough to offset that.

Another way to invest is to purchase a home or business. Many people have success with real estate, either flipping homes for a profit or renting them out. There are many tax advantages but also potentially many headaches. You have to do your homework. Again though, for many people it's better than the stock market.

A business purchase could be another great investment. I once had a friend suggest we should go together to buy a golf course to which I replied, "If you want to play golf, we'd need to buy a bowling alley." The reason being that we would work hard through the winter so we could enjoy summers playing golf. It's rarely a good idea to buy a business for the sole purpose of relaxation. Any hobby that becomes a business is usually no longer fun and could become drudgery. Don't get me wrong though. You don't want to get into a business that you wouldn't enjoy. There will most likely be long hours and some tough times. Your desire and passion hopefully will get you past those difficulties.

Another great consideration is to come up with an idea to create passive income. That's income that works for you. As an example, some people write a book and later add an online class that corresponds to the book. They may also get paid to speak. However, their speaking will always be limited to the number of hours in a day, whereas they can sell books or online classes while they sleep or take time off. That's passive income. The same could be said for a landlord or business owner. They'll create income whether they go to the office or not. But again, they'll have maintenance or guidance to give.

Some people aren't wired for the above examples, and if that's you, don't jump into a profession like that if you can't commit to the hours. However, if you get excited about the possibility of an unlimited income and accept the responsibility then go ahead and explore it.

The same could be said about sales careers in some ways. The only advice I'd give there though is to be careful about what type of sales career you got into. It needs to be a reputable company selling a quality product. Many times, top salespeople earn high commissions but again make sure you know someone who is actually doing it and speak with them before committing to a life of rejections.

Summary

There are many ways to set yourself up for financial success. Begin by determining your net worth every January 1st. List everything you own as well as all of your debts. This means that if your house is worth $200,000, but you owe $100,000, that leaves a $100,000 net. Do the same for cars and other large valued items. You can summarize household items with one line. Also list your savings and other bank accounts, and subtract any debts like credit cards, loans of any kind, etc. Don't forget to include 401k's, etc.

The key is to see financial growth. It makes any pain you feel by delaying gratification worthwhile. Sure, the neighbors may be driving a shiny new car every year, but you'll be the one retiring ten years before them.

Next, make sure you know where your money is going. Whether it's by budgeting or knowing where every dollar is spent; this puts you in a position where you're able to evaluate the *musts* from the *wants*. I recommend always making an improvement each year. If it's not pay raise or a promotion, perhaps it's switching insurance companies or cutting down on cable tv services.

If you can bring the family in on these discussions, that's great. Your children may not learn this anywhere else, and so the sooner you can guide them to be financially responsible, the better. Believe me, they'll thank you for it. Also, it's a smart move for spouses to work together on finances in the event something happens to one of you. In addition, this is a common area for disagreement between married couples; usually it's because they aren't on the same page. If you work together you can potentially ward off tension.

If your employer offers a 401k, oftentimes they will also offer a match up to a certain amount. For me they matched 50 cents on the dollar up to six percent of my salary. Therefore, if I saved six percent it automatically became nine percent.

If my six percent amounted to $100, they were contributing another $50 as well. You'll never get that kind of guaranteed return on investment anywhere. Be sure to take advantage of it.

Once you've set up a 401k, start a Roth IRA. Again, this money is growing tax deferred until you withdraw it later in life. By then the assumption is you'll be in a smaller tax bracket. You can do this for both husband and wife.

Cut non-essential expenses like a landline, cable television, subscriptions, Showtime, Netflix, Hulu, and whatever else is out there. If you feel that you need them, sign up with a promotion in the winter, then cancel come spring / summer when you'll most likely be busy with outdoor activities.

Shop for other routine bills like insurance, propane, internet etc. I bought a propane tank that enabled me to shop for the best deal. Routinely I save $250 per year from what others are paying. In addition, because I have a nest egg built up in savings, I was able to raise my deductibles on my insurances and save another $250 per year.

When it was time to get a new air conditioner, I researched options. I settled on a water heat pump. At the time the cost was $6,500. I got a one-third rebate from the government on my taxes. A new unit was going to cost over $2,500 for just the air conditioner unit. By buying the heat pump and having the ability to heat our home in the winter and cool it in the summer I figured it paid for itself in three years. Now we have the option of heating with either unit, and cooling with the heat pump. Typically, the government incentives are to promote energy savings so you'd see other opportunities with storm windows, a new furnace, storm doors etc

Pay extra on your house payment when you can. You'll notice on a $850 payment, perhaps $300 of those goes towards interest, (depending on your rates and timing). If you can afford to pay the interest amount in addition (making it

$1,150), you can pay off a 30-year mortgage in 15 years. Any amount you can afford is a help.

Drive dependable used cars. There's probably no better savings than this one tip. Cars are the worst investment you can ever make, and yet they are a necessity. You can cut your losses by driving a five-year-old car.

Side Hustle

"Side hustle" has become a popular term recently. People are finding a hobby or something they don't mind doing to bring in some extra income. It could be an Uber driver, a food delivery person, etc. I know a man who has always been handy working on cars. He works when he wants to and makes enough money that he never has to make withdraws for expenses. Another friend started a handyman business serving anyone, but especially single women, doing odd jobs around the house. The point is anyone can make extra money if they have the desire. It can also be for a season, or as long as you enjoy it or need it.

I've always enjoyed golf. When I was first married, we didn't have much discretionary money so I became a golf league secretary. Being the golf league secretary enabled me to play at no charge in exchange for running the golf league. I probably did that for ten years. Then when my family came along time was more valuable and my income had increased to allow me that pleasure. Recently I was asked to again take this responsibility, and I did. My wife asked me why I agreed to the extra work. She pointed out that we have the income, and I don't need to do it. However, I know that I can do the work while watching TV. It's not a chore to me, and it doesn't seem like work. And the benefit is free golf. No matter what your hobbies or interests are, you may be able to find a way to enjoy it for less.

When it comes to side hustles, think of the three-legged stool. One leg represents your skills, another your passion, and the third leg is the ability to make money. If you are lacking in any one area you won't succeed. As an example, if you have skill and passion but no market you have a hobby. If you have a market and skill but no passion you'll be bored. If you have passion and market but no skill you'll fail.

In Zig Ziglar's book, *Over the Top,* he mentions that legal immigrants are four times more likely to become millionaires than people born here in the United States. He claims that while we have our problems as a country, immigrants focus on opportunity. They see a variety of jobs offered in any newspaper and many storefronts. They work hard, living frugally, saving their money. Many times, they work a second and even a third job. By the time they see the problems of financial distress that many Americans complain about it's too late. They've already succeeded and capitalized on the opportunities that many people take for granted.

Another thing to be careful of is listening to the news. If your tips are coming from the media, you are in trouble. Number one, if it's true, everyone else is hearing it at the same time. Number two, they sensationalize everything. Every day I hear, BREAKING NEWS. Every day there is some story that they feel the need to shout about, that you and I and 99% of the population can do nothing about. Don't let yourself get caught up in that.

This reminds me of a USA article that ran years ago when the DOW was in a downward spiral. The headline was, "Where will it End!" A full page of doom and gloom, showing how prosperous the economy looked months earlier and now it was all anyone could talk about. The ironic part of the story was however, that very day was the bottom. The market started an upswing the very day the media was telling us no end was in sight. TV viewing was high as well. Economist after economist was interviewed adding their two cents.

The key, either educate yourself or seek advice from a professional that you can trust. Interview them, interview several. Take notes, ask any question that comes to mind. Ask about their fees and how they earn a living. The best ones will educate you and hold nothing back. The ones I'd be concerned with is anyone promising things that sound too good to be true.

Markets will swing and sometimes swing wildly. It's been said you can't time the market and with that I'd agree. Slow and steady wins the race. However, the one piece of advice you must adhere to is sell high and buy low. Many people do just the opposite. They buy when everyone else is, high end, and sell or panic when things start to go south. If it is a reputable company, they will bounce back nine times out of ten. The term diversify, meaning to not put all your eggs in one basket, can be applied when investing in the market. By holding several parts of several companies, you can level out highs and lows. When I started investing in the 1980's it was theorized a ten percent return was normal. My returns were much higher on average because I went more of an aggressive route. There was a period of time from 1987 through 2001 that almost any stock made money and many thrived. Then when 9/11 happened, the market tanked and most of the markets lost half of their values. People panicked. It quickly recovered but many missed the opportunities because they were on the sidelines.

Something similar happened in 2008-2009 with the banking industry collapse. Stocks dropped overnight. I recall a friend buying $10,000 worth of Ford and $10,000 worth of GM because both were at all-time lows. The GM stock lost him the entire $10,000 but the Ford stock was worth $150,000 a year later. So, a net gain of $130,000.

Again, almost any stock purchase would have enabled you to double your money inside of a year. But you had to have some capital to invest, and be willing to speculate that a turnaround was coming.

I heard a speaker recently explaining there were 5,000 millionaires around 1900. By 2000 that number had climbed to 5,000,000. Currently there are over 8,000,000. It's been said most are first generation millionaires, meaning the money was earned, not inherited. That tells me there has never been a better time to be alive. The speaker was author Brian Tracy and he had 16 tips for becoming a millionaire. The one that especially resonated with me was this: *See yourself as self-employed.* It's especially true that being self-employed will drastically improve your chances of financial success. But this one tip really stood out.

There's no doubt in my mind if I had it to do over again, I'd have been an entrepreneur. I had a taste of it and while I thrived at it, I let the opportunity slip away looking for security. Little did I know that true security lies in your own hands. Luckily for me, though, I had several great jobs where I was able to act in a way that seemed like I was working for myself. Even in my entry level jobs I was entrusted to do what I was trained to do, and then some. I wanted to be constantly learning and enjoyed the opportunities. I felt it made the days go faster. Some people I worked with tried to convince me that I was being taken advantage of but I never gave in to that way of thinking.

Opportunities came my way and more chances to make improvements that I saw needed done. I recall one of my bosses pulling me aside and saying, "I have no ability to do what you do, I appreciate your knowledge and abilities, and I won't get in your way. I trust you. Do what you feel needs done and come see me if you run into an obstacle that I can help with." What an amazing pep talk. Do you think I was walking on cloud nine for a while? It included no pay raise but what a feeling it gave me to know that I was trusted to do anything I saw the need to improve.

By acting like you are self-employed, even if you aren't, you are looking for innovation, continuous improvement. Again, you may not be paid for your efforts in dollars, at least not initially but with this mindset it will pay off in the future with increased opportunities and promotions.

Basic mistakes people make:

1) Not saving for a rainy day, have an emergency fund
2) Taking on debt other than a house, (credit cards etc)
3) Buying too much house
4) Not having a budget
5) Not delaying gratification

Questions to consider: On a scale of 1 – 10 with 10 being perfection how would you rate yourself in this area? ____
Consider

1) Do I have debt? Is my debt limited to just my home, or do I have additional debts?
2) If I do have other debt, do I have a plan in place to have it paid off within 18 months?
3) Do I live on 70 to 80% of my income saving / investing / giving the balance?
4) If / when a bonus or extra income comes my way, is it saved or invested?
5) Do I have ample savings considering my age?

Takeaway:

- Live beneath your means, automate your savings, be grateful and share.
- When you get a pay increase it's ok to increase your lifestyle but not 100% of the raise. I'd suggest no more

than 25%, saving the 75%. The same for promotions, bonuses, etc.
- Shop for deals, stretching your dollar makes sense. I'm not advocating driving miles to save a nickel on gas, but be conscious of where your money is going. Everything from food to insurance, gas and more. Nothing is off limits. Conserve energy, reuse bent nails.
- Dave Ramsey especially goes against buying new cars, a used dependable car is much more affordable in the long run.
- Entertainment, vacations are great, but I always like the quote, instead of escaping your life on an expensive vacation, why not build a life you don't need to escape from. We can justify anything we want, but we all know kids want time with their parents, it needn't be costly.
- Jim Rohn suggested the 70-10-10-10 plan. Live on 70% save 10%, invest 10% give 10%.
- If you've messed up, take ownership, get a 2nd job, sell some stuff, get out of debt.
- Whatever you buy, make sure that when you get the bill, you're still happy

Don't worry about comparing yourself to others. If someone inherited some money or hit the lottery what does that have to do with you?

Start examining what's holding you back instead of how others got where they are. Look at what you're doing or not doing. That's all you can control anyway.

Study the experiences of others who earned their way to the top instead of being born there. Then when you arrive, you'll truly be deserving.

CHAPTER 7

FUN / JOY

Most folks are about as happy as they make up their minds to be.
-Abe Lincoln

When I first started thinking about the eight facets of life, my planner labeled the final category as "other." I don't know about you, but I don't like "other." It sounds like a catch all. I wanted to label the idea with something that had more meaning.

Initially I called this piece of our life "lifestyle" but finally settled on *fun*. It's what we do with our life in those rare instances when we have a moment.

Many would say *I never take time for myself*, which could likely be said of any parent with young children. You've also most likely heard *all work and no play makes Jack a dull boy*. The truth of the matter is we'll make time for the things we enjoy.

Things I'd categorize here are reading, woodworking, photography, travel, playing an instrument, fishing, golf, playing cards, board games, gardening, running, walking, tennis, bowling, knitting, crafts, and on and on. The key I believe is finding an activity that uses your mind and excites you. Things I would not include here would be passive activities like watching TV or scrolling social media.

Many of the things we do in this category might be detested by others. *How do you enjoy that, that seems like a waste of time*, someone might say? However just like beauty is in the eye of the beholder, hobbies fall into a similar mindset.

I have several hobbies that interest me. The one that is most time consuming is golf. This could be an example of someone criticizing a hobby as a waste of time. For me though it's enjoyable, (most of the time) it's an opportunity to unwind and enjoy nature. I'm getting exercise because I normally walk, it can be a relationship builder, thus a career enhancer and doesn't have to be expensive.

No matter what your hobbies are, if you can enjoy some time away from work and the daily responsibilities of life, you'll be more energized once returning. Some people even make money with their hobbies like woodworking etc.

In many cases the more time spent on a hobby, eventually it's not a hobby anymore. That's ok, our interests change over time. I think it's a big benefit to involve your spouse/children if possible. It's not to say it's a must but it can be rewarding for some. Plus, if it's enjoyed by others, you won't feel guilty being away from your family. However, I'd discourage forcing your hobbies on them. It's better to introduce them, and if they too enjoy it, have them suggest it to you.

I mentioned that this is an area that's easily neglected. In certain seasons of our life that's expected. I recall the year we built our house, I played golf once the entire year. Anyone that knows me, knows that was a sacrifice. Additionally, when our boys were young and played T-ball and other activities, I never committed to a league but played only when other responsibilities were first taken care of.

Let me expand on how hobbies needn't be expensive. When I was young, I didn't want to spend a lot of money on golf, yet I wanted to play. I'd heard a local course allowed the league secretary a free membership in turn for the responsibility of running the league. I don't recall if I asked or he heard I was interested, at any rate he was burned out and offered me the opportunity.

For several years I enjoyed all the golf I wanted at no expense to my budget. At the same time I did not feel that I was taking income away from my family either. It's not to say I didn't have to earn it. I had to review score cards and calculate handicaps and post weekly results. The whole process probably took five hours to set up and an hour or so per week to maintain.

Since this time some courses only offer free play for the night your league plays rather than a free membership but that's just an example of how a hobby doesn't need to be expensive, especially if you're just starting out. I've offered this advice to others be it swimming or tennis or whatever. Many times, the person just shrugs their shoulders as if to say why would they allow me to do that? Which means you'll never get an opportunity if you don't ask.

I've known people who enjoy woodworking or auto repair and actually make a lot of money on the side. Some people garden and offer their excess produce to others be it for free or a small fee. The point is hobbies not only needn't be expensive, sometimes they can be downright lucrative.

Happiness

Happiness is the precursor to success. Most people think it's the other way around. Here are a few stats I go from The Happiness Advantage by Shawn Achor. A survey done in 2010 showed 45% of workers were happy with their jobs, the lowest in 22 years. Depression rates are ten times higher than 1960. Fifty years ago, the average age of a person treated for depression was 29.5. Today it's 14.5

So, what's the problem? It seems there's a huge focus on negativity in my mind. In addition, so many people feel overwhelmed many of us think it's normal. Shawn points out in his book that as a society we know very well how to be unwell and miserable and so little about how to thrive.

His field he describes as positive psychology and I recall him in a speech once saying that in standard psychology people had a problem, and went to the doctor only to find out they had ten problems. This did two things, it got to the root of the problem and it also kept them coming back for many more sessions. In the end however the goal was to bring them to normal or average.

The difference he says of positive psychology is, here they study the elite of the elite. The top athletes, top business professionals, top of any category and take what they can in an effort to share with the masses, thus bringing the entire average higher. That in a nutshell is exactly what I've tried to accomplish in writing this book.

He shares seven principles that fuel success and performance at work but I'd go so far as to say success in life as well. It is definitely worth buying.

A great story I once heard was about a woman who enjoyed painting. Others told her it's fine to do that as a youngster, but you'll need to learn some skills like typing and filing to support yourself. She did just that as well as helping out around the farm.

She worked for a neighboring farm as a live-in maid for 15 years where she met and married a farm hand at the age of 27. They had ten children--of which 5 survived--as they moved from farm to farm. She supplemented the family income selling potato chips and churning butter. This was the early 1900's. Her husband died of a heart attack in 1927 and her son helped her operate the farm for another nine years. She retired and moved in with her daughter in 1936. She had enjoyed embroidery and made and sold many items earlier but by now had developed arthritis at the age of 76, and it was too painful to continue.

At the age of 78 she began painting again at the prompting of her sister. Her hands still hurt so she began painting left-handed. Her initial works were displayed and sold at a local merchant for $3-5. An art collector bought all that were on display. He shared them with others and her popularity spread.

Anna Mary died in 1961 at the age of 101, but was dubbed Grandma Moses and the name stuck. Her most famous painting sold for 1.2 million dollars in 2006. She painted hundreds of pictures from memory. Not bad for a woman who was told she needed to learn some life skills. It was estimated she painted over 1,600 paintings, 25 of them after turning 100.

Most likely our hobbies can't produce millions of dollars like Grandma Moses. Nonetheless, as we experience all life has to offer, perhaps we can feel like a million bucks when enjoying our down time.

I heard of a study that was done that involved 180 nuns. They kept diaries or journals their entire life. These writings were studied looking for levels of happiness based on optimism as well as other factors. It was determined the nuns who were most content with life and had more optimism lived on average ten years longer. That amazed me but it didn't surprise me. I figured the lifespan would be longer but not ten years. This study in itself should encourage us to look for the positives in life and look for the silver linings in situations.

I recall a couple stories that Jim Rohn shared concerning happiness. The first was a man that attended one of his seminars. After listening to the talk, he decided he needed to make some changes. The man had two daughters and felt he had been treating them unfairly. He always was grumpy when they wanted to do things yet they gave him no reason to not trust them. They were good students, helped around the house and had great manners.

He decided from this day forth I'm going to be a better dad. He knew a favorite band they enjoyed listening to was coming to town. He bought them tickets before they ever asked to attend. In addition, he paid for them and decided to surprise them that very night.

When he arrived home, he told the two girls he had a surprise. He had learned something about himself earlier in the day and wanted to express his appreciation for having such two great daughters. He then gave them the tickets. Naturally they were speechless to say the least.

The best part however was when they arrived at the concert and presented their tickets to the usher and he started them down the aisle. They got closer and closer to the stage and they thought certainly there must be a mistake. But there wasn't. Dad had gotten them front and center. You can imagine their joy and it lasted all night including when they arrived home and thanked their father profusely. Needless to say, he was glad he made the commitment to change his ways.

Another story he shared had to do with an experience he had. He was with his lady friend and they decided to take a drive along the Pacific and take in the sites. They visited a town along the way and he stopped at a florist to buy a single rose. He then presented the rose to his friend so she could carry it as they walked and visited the local shops. She had commented she hadn't seen anyone else carrying a rose. Imagine how special she felt and only at the cost of a dollar or two.

They then stopped for gas at a time when attendants filled your tank. Jim explained they were visitors to the area and he wondered if there was a place nearby to get a milkshake. The attendant said, there sure is and they are great, and instructed him how to get there. Jim paid for his gas and the attendant added that when you park, make sure you park at the side to avoid the busy street and any potential mishaps. Jim thanked him and remarked to his friend what a pleasant young man they had just had the experience of being served by.

They got their milkshakes and while there got an extra one. When leaving town, they stopped by the gas station and the young man came out to serve them. Realizing who it was he said, I see you got your milkshakes, to which Jim said, indeed we did, and here's one for you. We wanted to thank you for your excellent service. The young man said wow, for me, no one has ever done that before.

As they drove away Jim looked in his rear view and watched the young man wave goodbye, milkshake in hand. All that joy for the cost of a couple dollars.

Serving others brings joy. In addition, as you recall those memories you get to experience them again.

Many times, we think I'll be happy when _____ (you fill in the blank). I heard of a man who categorized life in stages. The first stage was stuff. It was the necessities of life, your house, car etc. The second stage was different stuff. This might be a bigger house, nicer car, maybe a boat as well. Then came different stuff. By now he had become wealthy and was a part owner of a professional football team. Certainly, entertaining his friends in a luxury box would make him happy.

Finally, a friend asked him to accompany him on a trip to Bosnia. They were delivering wheelchairs to children who had lost their ability to walk, because of playing in mine fields in the war-torn country. As he placed a child in the first wheelchair the boy wouldn't let go. Through an interpreter the boy said, "I want to look into your face a little while longer, so when we meet again in heaven, I'll recognize you."

That's when he discovered the fourth stage. A life of purpose. Since that trip the man has gone on to start his own foundation and delivered over 40,000 more wheelchairs and counting.

Books I've read that support:

The Happiness Advantage, Out Live Your Life
Happiness is based on happenings and events, joy is deeper

I recall an article that suggested people think they need rest in order to rejuvenate but studies show we are more energized by more activity. We might think downtime means sitting on the couch and watching tv binge watching Netflix. Nothing could be further from the truth. In studies conducted people felt better about themselves and better about returning to work after a weekend that they attended to things that needed done.

This could be a project that they'd been putting off or starting an exercise routine. It might have been visiting a friend or relative that you hadn't seen in a while. Anything you do will motivate you and give you a better feeling about yourself than simply crashing on your couch.

Basic mistakes people make:

1) Not making time for fun or joy
2) Making too much time for fun or joy
3) Feeling guilty when getting the time to enjoy yourself (especially if married and even more so if children)
4) Comparing your joy to others
5) Listening to others suggestions and implementing if not yours

Questions to consider: On a scale of 1 – 10 with 10 being perfection how would you rate yourself in this area? ____

Consider

1) When I make time for joy am I able to present in the moment?

2) Do I allow ample time in my schedule for joy? (Again, if married this is a 2-way street)
3) Even if I can't partake in my favorite activity is there another way I can re-energize?
4) Do you take the pity approach? We'll make time for what we enjoy or feel is important

Takeaway:

- Hobbies needn't be expensive. They also could change over time. Your kids when they are young are just as likely to remember the nature walks you took, or sledding down a hill at a park as they would an expensive Disney vacation.
- If you'd like more information on any hobby the best place to start is any magazine or website on that particular subject. For example, I look at Golf and Golf Digest magazines sites to learn more about my favorite hobby.
- Another place is your local library, they too have most magazines, as well as many books or dvds
- I recall reading somewhere that fun (pleasure) is what we experience during an act; happiness is what we experience after an act. It is a deeper, more abiding emotion. It seems therefore we can bring happiness into our lives simply by recalling something from our past. Happiness is a by-product of who you are and what you do.
- I approached our local newspaper over four years ago suggesting I write a weekly column. I submitted some samples and they agreed. I get periodic emails from readers and many comments in person of how much people appreciate my articles. Many are my own, some

are just interesting things I've read. I'm no writer, I just have taken the time to try and others' feedback keeps me going. What makes you come alive? Try it yourself

- Maybe happiness is a better category than fun! What do you think?

CHAPTER 8

FAITH

Man gives advice, God gives guidance.

In my diagram of the *Eight Facets of Life*, you'll notice faith is at the bottom. My logic for placing it there is, it's the foundation of our lives, or at least it should be in my opinion. I didn't always understand this, but once I did it has made all the difference for me.

I've been sharing the eight facets with others for a few years now. In all my teachings, when asking participants which of the eight facets were the most important, faith always comes out on top. That's not to say that everyone agrees, but collectively faith is always most important.

I haven't always felt this way. I'm ashamed to admit it, but I just never understood faith years ago. I always thought it was right to put family first. After all I helped bring these children into the world, what loving father wouldn't look out for them? Then I realized that's exactly what God has done for us. He brought us into this world and gives us every good thing we experience. If I choose to serve Him first, why wouldn't He in turn bless me? Don't mistake my using the term blessings, as a life with no problems. It's a matter of getting our priorities in order.

I've learned a lot about faith, and I learn more every day. God reveals things to me constantly. I read His word and ponder *How does this apply to me?* I used to use words like *coincidence, ironic,* and phrases like *isn't that something, the way that worked out?* Not anymore! The more I study, and the closer I get to God, the more I see and realize His hand is in everything.

I heard a preacher once say, "It's our responsibility to challenge a thirsty world." I really believe this is a major problem with society. We are all thirsty, but mistake that thirst for worldly pleasures. To one it might be fame and status in a job, to another the size of our portfolio. Some people make their God, their family, or their relationships. Someone else might be so far into their health, there is nothing more important. Finally, some might think fun is what life is all about, and like King Solomon found out it's like chasing the wind. Fun today isn't fun tomorrow. It could be alcohol, drugs, pornography and on and on.

The thirst we feel is God calling us to Him. He's planted that desire to know Him personally. Satan takes that thirst and confuses us into thinking it's something else. If we'd just do this or chase that for a while, then we'd be happy.

The Lord wants us to walk wisely so that we can enjoy all of the marvelous benefits that He has promised in His Word and longs to give us. Wasted opportunities and time misspent can never be reclaimed. We need to commit to make each and every day count for Jesus Christ instead of merely living for ourselves.

I recall hearing of a group of pilots that made regular flights in Africa. The flight took an hour and never deviated. However, on this particular day their instruments indicated they'd arrived in 20 minutes. Figuring this was impossible they continued flying and flew another 40 minutes into the Sahara Desert where they all perished. The Bible can be compared to our instruments. It's the truth.

I heard a story of a man who was a runner. He wasn't a world class runner, but he enjoyed it. He even ran in some races. Additionally, he subscribed to three runner's magazines. He enjoyed reading them and felt a connection. At one point he sustained an injury that kept him from running for a period of months. He found that since he couldn't run, he lost his interest in reading about it as well, and so he lost his connection.

How does this story parallel our own Bible reading? If you're not running the race, the Bible won't appeal to you either.

I've heard people say *I didn't get anything out of today's sermon*. (I might have been guilty of that as well, in the past). However, we need to ask ourselves, *what did we put into it?* The preacher or the speaker is just the messenger. We have a responsibility to connect as well.

If you don't already have a good study Bible, get one. I use the *New Living Translation Life Application Study Bible* myself and have found it to be most useful. There are so many footnotes to help me understand the meaning behind the meaning. It's important to also consider how God will speak to you if you are only using an author's footnotes to clarify your understanding. I still like the footnotes though to help me see or think in a way I perhaps didn't understand before. We all need to take time in prayer as well.

Another tip is to get into the habit of reading daily devotions. Most are free. We have *In Touch* mailed to our home but also subscribe to three or four more via e-mail. Many times, the daily reading is a source for discussion between my wife and me.

One thing that enabled me to learn about faith at an accelerated pace was when I joined a Sunday School class. Sermons are great, but usually a sermon is like a lecture, whereas a Sunday School class gives you the opportunity to ask questions and hear other's thoughts as well. To learn at an even more accelerated pace, offer to teach a Sunday School class. You study the lesson, then get the benefit of hearing everyone else's thoughts when it's covered in class.

I grew up as an Easter / Christmas church-goer. That's when we would go to church as a family. I did go once in a while with friends. They may have a bring-a-friend-to-church day, so I'd get asked. My experience, however, wasn't the best. When attending with friends my goal was to show up and listen but I recall getting called on, and that seemed unfair because I wasn't a regular. The others had the advantage of hearing or being trained in a way that I didn't. I felt uncomfortable. I imagine now, looking back, the teacher was probably trying to include me in the conversation.

The feeling I got in hanging around friends that went to church regularly was that they were no different than me. We used the same language and shared the same ideas so early on I saw no difference in going to church as not going to church.

I did have the benefit of a program in elementary school called Weekday Religious Education. It was a traveling trailer that visited county schools and reached out to all children to let them know that God loved them. It was one hour once per week. It was voluntary, but as far as I knew, everyone attended. That training gave me a little insight into God's presence and must have made an impact because I still remember several stories told and lessons shared.

My wife and I decided to get married around the age of 21. We didn't want to be hypocrites and get married in a church but not be members of the congregation, so about six months prior to the date, we started attending. My then-fiancé was a regular attendee, but I only went when I couldn't play golf due to weather. In my mind I justified this was okay. I used to go a couple times per year, and now I was going about half the time or 26 times per year.

One of those times I was there I felt convicted that although 26 is better than two, God wanted all of me. I've since become a 52 week per year attendee. After a few years we had a son and as he grew, we decided to start going to Sunday School.

When we started going to church, we had a few couples invite us to Sunday School, but I thought we should ease into it. When I was finally ready to join the class, it was finished. What had been a group of 12-15 young adults worshiping and studying together was down to a teacher and me, and sometimes one more. That didn't lead to a great class. I hung with it as I was bringing our son, and I wasn't going to be that dad who drops his kid off and leaves.

As time went on our class grew and, eventually, we had a new preacher come that took over teaching. He was phenomenal, the closest thing to Billy Graham I could imagine. I learned so much those next ten years. I recall looking at his Bible, and it was held together with layers of tape. The pages were worn and had many notes written in the columns. In my childhood home we had a nice Bible on the coffee table, but I don't recall anyone ever looking at it. If something got placed on it, Mom was quick to point out the mistake. From this, I learned the Bible was sacred. However, looking at the preachers Bible, it was clear he meant it to be used as a tool. I soon adopted that way of thinking as well. I have highlights, notes in pen and pencil, as well as dog eared pages in my Bible now.

Our class grew to 12-15 people and had many great discussions that led to learning at an accelerated rate. Sermons are great, but they are a lecture; it's a one-sided message. In my experience in Sunday School, material is read or presented, then an open discussion typically takes place. Many times, I have found that someone else had a question that I was debating about asking as well. You get the benefit of the teacher's knowledge as well as everyone else in a discussion.

We grow up with a set of values, an idea of what's right and wrong from our parents, friends, and material we have studied or learned. One day in Sunday School we were discussing abortion. Everyone agreed this is against God's will. One person added that he couldn't understand how some people could be so pro-life on the abortion issue yet think capital punishment was perfectly okay. I swallowed hard. I had always felt this way, the way he described, and now my beliefs were being challenged. The more I thought about his stance I realized it had merit, although I still thought my thoughts did as well. Didn't the Bible say *an eye for an eye and a tooth for a tooth* I reasoned? Then I found out the meaning behind the eye and the tooth story--It was to ensure people didn't go beyond just punishment. Furthermore, when Jesus walked the earth, his teachings were all about forgiveness and turning the other cheek.

Life is life whether it's an unborn baby or a criminal. It's a stance I'd never have considered changing unless I heard this one man's opinion, and after much thought and searching the Bible, I decided to adopt this way of thinking myself.

We might reason that if someone kidnapped our child and killed him, we would demand justice. Yet we've also heard how someone, despite his grief, forgave the criminal and, in some cases, even gave witness to them. I cannot imagine going through such pain and having a forgiving spirit, but it's what Jesus would do.

As our class continued to grow our preacher suggested that perhaps we should break into two classes. He felt and studies confirm that when groups get above 10-12 you lose some intimacy; people don't talk as much. I took the hint and started another class, reaching out to people that either weren't coming to Sunday School or weren't regular church-goers.

I recall an older woman telling me that my learning would deepen even more from teaching. "As a teacher," she explained, "you'll study your material, then present it, and receive others' feedback. It will be as if you've covered the material three times." I can confirm that has indeed been the case, and I've been blessed with opportunities.

Another benefit I never considered from being a part of a church came from being on various boards and leadership positions. Churches operate just like a business. I was blessed to observe our preacher's behavior during meetings. He always had a set agenda and stuck to it. If someone brought an additional item to a meeting that wasn't on the agenda, he politely declined to discuss it. This allowed meetings to keep moving along in a timely manner. Meetings always began on time, regardless of who was missing.

There is a saying that you don't realize what you have until it's gone, and it's what comes to mind when I think of this particular preacher. I knew he was organized, prepared and fair. For over twelve years as our minister, he led meetings as described. I have since been around many preachers and none have been able to make an hour-long meeting last less than two hours.

I have had the opportunity to fill in for preachers while they were on vacation or sick at several churches, including my own home church. I have always tried to do my part studying and preparing the message I was going to give, but each time I felt the Holy Spirit was there with me. I would be in the habit of making some notes and attempting to speak from the heart. Almost always God has brought something to me to add. It's usually something I have read elsewhere but didn't have it in my notes. Yet it fit perfect with the message I was led to share that day.

Following is a story I first read being passed along the Internet many years ago. It hit me at a time when one of my son's was young, and I couldn't help thinking of him as I read it. I think this story shares what God must feel like daily because of our lukewarm attitudes towards him.

It's a Tuesday night and you've made it home for dinner with your family, on time no less. After dinner you hear some news of a village in Africa that's been wiped out with a mystery illness. Turns out a couple of people contracted it weeks earlier and died but two deaths in a foreign country doesn't make news. Hundreds however does.

Later that week there are cases turning up in other countries. Some close their borders in an effort to keep this mystery illness contained. It seems people are contracting it with no symptoms showing up for a week, then they are dead in four days. The death toll reaches thousands.

The following week there are cases in Europe. The news people are going crazy. This is spreading and worse, yet we have no idea of how to stop it. Finally, two weeks after first hearing about this there are cases in the United States. Every day new reports of different states with confirmed cases. The death toll is now hundreds of thousands.

Finally, some doctors and researchers have broken the code. They feel a vaccine can be made but it's going to take the blood of someone who hasn't been infected. All throughout the Midwest everyone is asked to go to your local hospital and have your blood tested.

You do as you're told and take your family to the hospital. It's a Friday night and there is a long line. They've got nurses and doctors coming out and pricking fingers, taking blood and putting labels on it. Your wife and kids are there as well and as you are tested, they advise you to wait patiently while the samples are tested.

You stand around waiting to be dismissed with your neighbors. Everyone is scared, wondering what the world is going on and if this is the end of the world. Suddenly a young man comes running out of the hospital screaming. He's yelling a name and waving a clipboard.

What? He yells it again! And your son tugs on your jacket and says, "Daddy, that's me." Before you know it, they've grabbed your boy. Wait a minute, hold on! They say

"It's ok, his blood is clean. His blood is pure. We need to confirm with more tests he doesn't have the disease.

Five tense minutes later out comes the doctors and nurses, crying and hugging one another, some are even laughing. It's the first time you've seen anyone this happy in days. An older doctor approaches you and says, "thank you sir, your son's blood is perfect. It's clean, it's pure. We can make the vaccine.

As the word begins to spread around the parking lot people are screaming and praying and laughing and crying.

But then the doctor pulls you and your wife aside and says, "we didn't realize that the donor would be a minor and we need …. we need you to sign a consent form." You begin to sign then you notice that the number of pints of blood to be taken is empty. You ask, how many pints?

And that's when the doctor's smile fades and he said, "We had no idea it would be a child; we weren't prepared. We need it all!" You stammer, but, but, before you say anything the doctor says, "we're talking about the world here. Please sign it. We need it all.

But can't you give him a transfusion you ask? The doctor replies if we had clean blood, we could but there's none. Can you sign it? Would you sign it? In a numb silence you do.

Then they ask you if you'd like to have a moment with him before we begin? Can you? Can you walk back to the room where he's sitting asking, "Daddy, Mommy, what's going on?" Can you take his hand and say, "Son, your mommy and I love you and we never let anything happen to you that didn't just have to be? Do you understand that?

Soon the doctor comes in the room and says, "I'm sorry, we have to get started, people all over the world are dying." Can you leave. Can you walk out while he's saying, "Dad, Mom, why have you forsaken me?"

Then next week, when they have a ceremony to honor your son, some people choose to sleep in. Others are at the lake or the golf course. While some are there just pretending to care.

Wouldn't you want to jump up and say, "MY SON DIED FOR YOU! DON'T YOU CARE?"

Is that what God wants to say? My son died for you; don't you know how much I care?

When we attempt to see it from God's eyes our hearts are broken. Maybe now, we can begin to comprehend the great love you have for us.

That story had a profound effect on me. Like I mentioned, perhaps a part of it was because at the time I read it I had a son that was around eight years old. I could only imagine the agony of making a decision like that. Yet that's exactly what God has done for us. He gave up His Son so that we may have life. Yet many don't seem to care. Maybe they don't understand. Maybe they are too busy.

Basic mistakes people make:

1) Not going to church
2) Going to church, but not being present
3) Going to church, but thinking the message always applies to everyone else
4) Saying, "I'll get started tomorrow."
5) Saying, "I'd go but they are all a bunch of hypocrites."

Questions to consider: On a scale of 1 – 10 with 10 being perfection how would you rate yourself in this area? ____

Consider

1) We attend regularly and are active in our church.
2) I read devotions and or the Bible daily.
3) I attempt to apply what I learn.
4) I pray daily and give thanks for all God does.

5) I participate in a Bible study group and/or Sunday School.

Takeaway:

- Get into a good Bible-based Church. Get around fellow followers; learn and share. Never look down on others. Leave judgement up to God, only He knows the heart.
- In addition to reading the Bible, read other faith-based books. Many people write great stories that supplement scripture and give us something to think about. A few of my favorites are Max Lucado's *Outlive Your Life*, Kyle Idleman's *Not a Fan*, and Joeseph Girzone's *Joshua*.
- Remember the church isn't just a building, it's a community.
- I once heard someone ask, "Why do I need to go to church? I can study the Bible on my own." The best answer: Think of a campfire. The fire burns brightest when all the logs are together. Pull one aside, and, by itself, it will burn out. We need each other.
- Going to church doesn't make me a Christian any more than sitting in my garage makes me a car. Go to church, **then** apply what you learn.
- God has wired his world for power, but he calls on us to flip the switch.

Recently I came across some information on YouTube that is the best thing I've ever found regarding Bible teaching. This goes for any age or experience level as well. It's called The Bible Project. Be sure to check it out. Most segments ate 5-7 minutes in length and narrated with some amazing sketches.

Some of my favorite preachers on the internet are:

James Merritt www.touchinglives.com
Kyle idleman www.southeastchristianchurch.com
David Jeremiah www.davidjerimiah.org
Charles Stanley www.Intouch.com
and a Bible resource www.biblegateway.com

Christians need to be careful not to criticize others, especially other Christians. Focus on the similarities not the differences.

I recall a story of a statue in Germany of Jesus with his hands blown off by a bomb during World War II. Instead of repairing it, the residents added a plaque reading, "Christ hath no hands but yours. God needs our hands to complete His tasks on Earth."

Faith is such an important piece to the life puzzle, so I am adding additional material / stories that I have read over the years that have struck a chord. Therefore, if a name is associated with the article, I'll include it, otherwise it will be blank. These are not my words but words I felt help make a point. Enjoy.

A Brother Like That (Author Unknown)

A man named Paul received an automobile from his brother as a Christmas present. On Christmas Eve when Paul came out of his office, a street urchin was walking around the shining new car admiring it. "Is this your car, mister?" he asked.

Paul nodded. "My brother gave it to me for Christmas." The boy was astounded. "You mean your brother gave it to you and it didn't cost you nothing? Boy I wish ..." He hesitated.

Of course, Paul knew what he was going to ask for. He was going to wish he had a brother like that. But what the lad said jarred Paul all the way down to his heels.

"I wish," the boy went on, "that I could be a brother like that."

Paul looked at the boy in astonishment, then impulsively he added, "Would you like to take a ride?"

"Sure, I'd love that." After a short ride, the boy turned with his eyes aglow and said, "Mister, would you mind driving in front of my house?"

Paul smiled a little. He thought he knew what the lad wanted. He wanted to show his neighbors that he could ride home in a new automobile. But Paul was wrong again. "Will you stop where those two steps are?" the boy asked.

He ran up the steps. Then in a little while Paul heard him coming back, but he was not coming fast. He was carrying his little crippled brother. He sat him down on the bottom step, then squeezed up against him and pointed to the car.

"There she is, Buddy, just like I told you upstairs. His brother gave it to him for Christmas and it didn't cost him a cent. And someday I'm gonna give you one just like it… and you can see for yourself all the neat things in the Christmas windows that I've been trying to tell you about."

Paul got out and lifted the lad into the front seat of his car. The shining-eyed older brother climbed in beside him and the three of them began a memorable holiday ride.

That Christmas Eve, Paul learned what Jesus meant when he said, "It's more blessed to give…"

Mercy and Grace

Dr. Christianson, a professor of religion at a small college in western U.S., was a studious man. He taught the required survey course in Christianity. Every student was required to take his course during freshman year regardless of his or her major. Although Dr. Christianson tried hard to communicate the essence of the gospel in his class, he found that most of the students looked upon the course as nothing but required drudgery. Despite his best efforts, most students refused to take Christianity seriously.

This semester, Dr, Christianson had a special student named Steve. Steve was only a freshman, but was studying with the intent of going on to seminary. Steve was popular, well-liked, an imposing physical specimen and the starting center on the school football team. Steve was also the best student in the professor's class.

One day the professor asked Steve to stay after class. He asked Steve, "How many push-ups can you do?"

Steve said, "I do about 200 every night."

"Two hundred? That's pretty good, Steve," the professor said. "Do you think you could do 300?"

Steve replied, "I don't know, I've never done 300 at a time."

"Do you think you could?" again asked Dr. Christianson.

"Well, I can try," said Steve.

"Can you do 300 in sets of 10? I have a class project in mind and I need you to do about 300 push-ups in sets of ten for this to work. Can you, do it? I need you to tell me you can do it," said the professor.

Steve replied, "Well I think I can… yeah, I can do it."

Dr. Christianson said, "Good! I need you to do this on Friday. Let me explain what I have in mind…"

Friday came and Steve got to class early and sat in the front of the room. When class started, the professor pulled out a big box of donuts, not the normal kind, but the extra fancy BIG kind, with cream centers and frosting swirls. Everyone was excited it was Friday, the last class of the day, and they were going to get an early start on the weekend with a party in Dr. Christianson's class.

Dr. Christianson went to the first girl in the first row and asked, "Cynthia, do you want to have one of these donuts?"

Cynthia replied, "Yes."

The professor then turned to Steve and asked, "Steve, would you do ten push-ups so Cynthia can have a donut?"

Steve said, "Sure," and jumped down from his desk to do a quick ten, and returned to his seat. Dr. Christianson put a donut on Cynthia's desk.

The Dr. then went to Joe in the next seat and asked, "Joe do you want a donut?"

Joe said, "Yes."

Dr. Christianson asked, "Steve, would you do ten push-ups so Joe can have a donut?" Steve did ten push-ups; Joe got the donut. And so it went, down the first aisle, Steve did ten pushups for every person before they got their donut. And down the second aisle, till Dr. Christianson came to Scott. Scott was on the basketball team, and in as good condition as Steve. He was very popular and never lacking for female companionship. When the professor asked, "Scott do you want a donut?"

Scott's reply was, "Well can I do my own pushups?"

Dr. Christianson said, "No, Steve has to do them."

Then Scott said, "Well, I don't want one then."

Dr. Christianson shrugged and then turned to Steve and asked, "Steve, would you do ten pushups so Scott can have a donut he doesn't want?"

With perfect obedience Steve started to do ten pushups. Scott said, "HEY! I said I didn't want one!"

Dr Christianson said, "Look, this is my classroom, my class, my desks, and these are my donuts. Just leave it on the desk if you don't want it." And he put a donut on Scott's desk. By this time, Steve had begun to slow down a little. He just stayed on the floor between sets because it took too much effort to get up and down. You could start to see a little perspiration on his brow.

Dr. Christianson started down the third row. Now the students were beginning to get a little angry. Dr. Christianson asked Jenny, "Jenny, do you want a donut?"

Sternly, Jenny said, "No."

Dr Christianson asked Steve, "Steve, would you do ten more pushups so Jenny can have a donut that she doesn't want?" Steve did ten, Jenny got a donut.

By now a growing sense of uneasiness filled the room. The students were beginning to say *No* and there were all these uneaten donuts on the desks. Steve also had to really put forth a lot of extra effort to get these pushups done for each donut. There began to be a pool of sweat on the floor beneath his face, his arms and brow were beginning to get red because of the physical effort required.

Dr. Christianson asked Robert, who was the most vocal unbeliever in the class, to watch Steve do each push up to make sure he did the full ten pushups in a set because he couldn't bear to watch all of Steve's work for all those uneaten donuts. He sent Robert over to where Steve was so Robert could count the set and watch Steve closely. Dr. Christianson started down the fourth row.

During the class, however, some students from other classes had wandered in and sat down on the steps along the radiators that ran down the sides of the room. When the professor realized this, he did a quick count and saw there were now 34 students in the room. He started to worry if Steve would be able to make it.

Dr. Christianson went on to the next person and the next and the next. Near the end of that row, Steve was having a really rough time. He was taking a lot more time to complete each set. Steve asked Dr. Christianson, "Do I have to make my nose touch on each one?"

Dr. Christianson thought for a moment, "Well, they're your pushups. You are in charge now. You can do them any way you want." And Dr. Christianson went on.

A few moments later, Jason, a recent transfer student, came to the room and was about to come in when all the students yelled in one voice, "NO! Don't come in! Stay out!"

Jason didn't know what was going on. Steve picked up his head and said. "No, let him come."

Professor Christianson said, "You realize that if Jason comes in you will have to do ten pushups for him?"

Steve said, "Yes, let him come in. Give him a donut."

Dr. Christianson said, "Okay, Steve, I'll let you get Jason's out of the way right now. Jason, do you want a donut?"

Jason, new to the room, hardly knew what was going on. "Yes," he said, "give me a donut."

"Steve, will you do ten pushups so that Jason can have a donut?"

Steve did ten pushups very slowly and with great effort. Jason, bewildered, was handed a donut and sat down.

Dr. Christianson finished the fourth row, then started on those visitors seated by the heaters. Steve's arms were now shaking with each pushup in a struggle to lift himself against the force of gravity. Sweat was profusely dropping off of his face and by this time, there was no sound except his heavy breathing; there was not a dry eye in the room.

The very last two students in the room were two young women, both cheerleaders, and very popular. Dr. Christianson went to Linda, the second to last and said, "Linda, do you want a doughnut?"

Linda said, very sadly, "No, thank you."

Professor Christianson quietly asked, "Steve, would you do ten pushups so that Linda can have a donut she doesn't want?" Grunting from the effort, Steve did ten very slow pushups for Linda. Then Dr. Christianson turned to the last girl, Susan.

"Susan, do you want a donut?"

Susan, with tears flowing down her cheeks, began to cry. "Dr Christianson, why can't I help him?"

Dr. Christianson, with tears of his own, said, "No, Steve has to do it alone, I have given him this task and he is in charge of seeing that everyone has an opportunity for a donut whether they want it or not. When I decided to have a party this last day of class, I looked at my grade book. Steve is the only student with a perfect grade. Everyone else has failed a test, skipped a class, or offered me inferior work. Steve told me that in football practice, when a player messes up, he must do pushups. I told Steve that none of you could come to my party unless he paid the price by doing your pushups. He and I made a deal for your sakes. "Steve, would you do ten pushups so Susan can have a donut?" As Steve very slowly finished his last pushup, with the understanding that he had accomplished all that was required of him, having done 350 pushups, his arms buckled beneath him and he fell to the floor.

Dr. Christianson turned to the room and said, "And so it was that our Savior, Jesus Christ, on the cross pleaded to the Father, 'Into thy hands I commend my spirit.' With the understanding that he had done everything that was required of Him, he yielded up His life. And like some of those in this room, many of us leave the gift on the desk, uneaten."

Two students helped Steve up off the floor and to a seat, physically exhausted, but wearing a thin smile.

"Well done, good and faithful servant," said the professor. "Not all sermons are preached in words."

Turning to his class the professor said, "My wish is that you might understand and fully comprehend all the riches of grace and mercy that have been given to you through the sacrifice of our Lord and Savior Jesus Christ, who spared not the only Begotten Son, but gave Him up for us all, for the whole Church, now and forever."

Faith

* * *

After a few of the usual Sunday evening hymns, the church's pastor slowly stood up, walked over to the pulpit and, before he gave his sermon for the evening, briefly introduced a guest minister who was in the service that evening. In the introduction, the pastor told the congregation that the guest minister was one of his dearest childhood friends and that he wanted him to have a few moments to greet the church and share whatever he felt would be appropriate for the service. With that, an elderly man stepped up to the pulpit and began to speak.

"A father, his son, and a friend of his son were sailing off the Pacific coast," he began, "when a fast-approaching storm blocked any attempt to get back to the shore. The waves were so high, that even though the father was an experienced sailor, he could not keep the boat upright and the three were swept into the ocean as the boat capsized."

The old man hesitated for a moment, making eye contact with two teenagers who were, for the first time since the service began, looking somewhat interested in his story.

The aged minister continued, "Grabbing a rescue line, the father had to make the most excruciating decision of his life; to which boy would he throw the other end of the life line? He only had seconds to make the decision. The father knew that his son was a Christian, and he also knew that his son's friend was not. The agony of his decision could not be matched by the torrent of waves."

"As the father yelled out, 'I love you son!' he threw out the life line to his son's friend. By the time the father had pulled the friend back to the capsized boat, his son had disappeared. Beneath the raging swells into the black of the night. His body was never recovered."

By this time the two teenagers were sitting up straight in the pew, anxiously awaiting the next words to come out of the old minister's mouth.

"The father," he continued, "knew his son would step into eternity with Jesus, and he could not bear the thought of his son's friend stepping into an eternity without Jesus. Therefore, he sacrificed his son to save his son's friend."

"How great is the love of God that he should do the same for us? Our heavenly Father sacrificed his only begotten Son that we could be saved. I urge you to accept his offer to rescue you and take a hold of the life line he is throwing out to you in this service." With that, the old man turned and sat back down in his chair as silence filled the room.

The pastor again walked slowly to the pulpit and delivered a brief sermon with an invitation at the end. However, no one responded to the appeal.

Within minutes after the service ended, the two teenagers were at the old man's side. "That was a nice story," politely stated one of the boys. "But I don't think it was very realistic for a father to give up his only son's life in hope that the other boy would become a Christian."

"Well, you've got a point there," the old man replied, glancing down at his worn bible. A big smile broadened his face. He once again looked up at the boys and said, "It sure isn't very realistic, is it? But I'm standing here today to tell you that story gives me a glimpse of what it must have been like for God to give up his son for me. You see… I was that father and your pastor is my son's friend.

* * *

Here's one that's most likely familiar. It was attributed to a Notre Dame football player and a woman took credit for it. The format it came to me in said author unknown.

How to Live Your Dash

A man stood up to speak at the funeral of a friend. He referred to the dates on her tombstone from the beginning to the end.

> He noted that first came her date of birth and spoke the following date with tears.
> But said what mattered most of all was the dash between those years.
> For that dash represents all the time that she spent alive on earth
> And now only those who love her know what that little line was worth
> For it matters not how much we own, the cars, the house, the cash –
> What matters most is how we live and love and how we spend the dash.
> So, think about long and hard… are their things you'd like to change?
> For you never know how much time is left that can still be arranged.
> If we could just slow down enough to consider what is true and real
> And try to understand the way that other people feel.
> Be less quick to anger and show appreciation more,
> And love the people in our lives like we've never loved them before.
> Treat each other with respect and more often wear a smile,
> Remembering this special dash might only last a while.
> So, when your eulogy is being read, with your life's actions to rehash,
> Would you be proud of the things they say; about the way you spent your dash?

When I read this, it reminds me that no one knows their date for meeting God. And while this should be a warning for how we spend our time, most of us nod our heads in agreement, but before the day is over, we slip back into our routines. We say we are busy, but busy doing what?

Grandpa's Glasses

There once was a carpenter who was building some crates for the clothes that his church was sending to an orphanage in China. On his way home, he reached into his shirt pocket to get his glasses, but they were gone.

When he mentally replayed his earlier actions, he realized what had happened; the glasses had slipped out of his pocket unnoticed and fallen into one of the crates which he then nailed shut.

His brand-new glasses were heading to China! The Great Depression was at its height, and grandpa had six children. He had spent twenty dollars for those glasses that very morning. He was upset by the thought of having to buy another pair. "It's not fair," he told God as he drove home in frustration.

"I've been very faithful in giving my time and money to your work, and now this."

Several months later, the director of the orphanage was on furlough in the United States. He wanted to visit all the churches that had supported him in China, so he came to speak one Sunday at my grandfather's small church in Chicago.

The missionary began by thanking the people for their faithfulness in supporting the orphanage. "But most of all," he said, "I must thank you for the glasses you sent last year. You see, enemy soldiers had just swept through the orphanage, destroying everything, including my glasses. I was desperate. Even if I had the money, there was simply no way of replacing those glasses. Along with not being able to see so well, I experienced headaches every day, so my co-workers and I were much in prayer about this.

Then your crates arrived. When my staff removed the covers, they found a pair of glasses laying on top. The missionary paused long enough to let his words sink in. Then, still gripped with the wonder of it all, he continued: "Folks, when I tried on those glasses, it was as though they had been custom-made just for me! I want to thank you for being a part of that."

The people listened, happy for the miraculous glasses. But the missionary surely must have confused their church with another, so they thought. There were no glasses on their list of items to be sent overseas. But sitting quietly in the back, with tears streaming down his face, an ordinary carpenter realized the Master Carpenter had used him in an extraordinary way.

Wow, what a story. Have you ever lost something, maybe a five-dollar bill, or a ten, twenty or more? Maybe a way to look at it in the future is, instead of beating yourself up, choose to believe that the person who finds it is in desperate need. You'll most likely never know but look how this story worked out. God can work in miraculous ways.

Why Christmas?

There was once a man who didn't believe in God, and he didn't hesitate to let others know how he felt about religion and religious holidays, like Christmas.

His wife, however, did believe, and she raised their children to also have faith in God and Jesus, despite his disparaging comments.

One snowy Christmas Eve, his wife was taking their children to a Christmas Eve service in the farm community in which they lived. She asked him to come but he refused. "That story is nonsense!" he said. "Why would God lower Himself to come to earth as a man? That's ridiculous!"

So, she and the children left, and he stayed home. A while later, the winds grew stronger and the snow turned into a blizzard. As the man looked out the window, all he saw was a blinding snowstorm. He sat down to relax before the fire for the evening.

Then he heard a loud thump. Something had hit the window. Then another thump. He looked out, but couldn't see more than a few feet. When the snow let up a little, he ventured outside to see what could have been beating on his window. In the field near his house, he saw a flock of wild geese.

Apparently, they had been flying south for the winter when they got caught in the snow storm and couldn't go on. They were lost and stranded on his farm, with no food or shelter. They just flapped their wings and flew around the field in low circles, blindly and aimlessly. A couple of them had flown into his window, it seemed.

The man felt sorry for the geese and wanted to help them. The barn would be a great place for them to stay, he thought. It is warm and safe; surely, they could spend the night and wait out the storm. So he walked over to the barn and opened the doors wide, then watched and waited, hoping they would notice the open barn and go inside. But the geese just fluttered around aimlessly and did not seem to notice the barn or realize what it could mean for them.

The man tried to get their attention, but that just seemed to scare them, and they moved further away. He went into the house and came back with some bread, broke it up, and made a breadcrumb trail leading to the barn. They still didn't catch on.

Now he was getting frustrated. He got behind them and tried to shoo them toward the barn, but they only got more scared and scattered in every direction except toward the barn. Nothing he did could get them to go into the barn where they would be warm and safe.

"Why don't they follow me?" he exclaimed. "Can't they see this is the only place they'll survive the storm?" He thought for a moment and realized that they just wouldn't follow a human. "If only I were a goose, then I could save them," he said out loud.

Then he had an idea. He went into the barn, got one of his own geese, and carried it in his arms as he circled around behind the flock of wild geese. He then released it. His goose flew through the flock and straight into the barn, and one by one the other geese followed to safety.

He stood silently for a moment as the words he had spoken a few minutes earlier replayed in his mind; "If only I were a goose, then I could save them!" Then he thought about what he had said to his wife earlier. "Why would God want to be like us? That's ridiculous!"

Suddenly it all made sense. That is exactly what God has done for us. We are like the geese, blind, lost, perishing. God had his Son become like us so He could show us the way and save us. That was the meaning of Christmas he realized.

As the winds and blinding snow died down, his soul became quiet as he pondered this wonderful thought. Suddenly he understood what Christmas (Christ) was all about and why HE had come. Years of doubt and disbelief vanished like the passing storm.

He fell to his knees in the snow, and prayed his first prayer: "Thank you, God, for coming in human form to get me out of the storm!"

Death (A wonderful way to explain it)

A sick man turned to his doctor as he was preparing to leave the examination room and said, "Doctor, I am afraid to die. Tell me what lies on the other side?"

Very quietly the doctor said, "I don't know."

"You don't know? You're a Christian man, and don't know what's on the other side?"

The doctor was holding the handle of the door; On the other side came a sound of scratching and whining, and as he opened the door, a dog sprang into the room and leaped on him with an eager show of gladness. Turning to the patient, the doctor said, "Did you notice my dog? He's never been in this room before. He didn't know what was inside. He knew nothing except his master was here, and when the door opened, he sprang in without fear. I know little of what is on the other side of death, but I do know one thing... I know my Master is there and that is enough!"

CONCLUSION

I'd like to attempt to summarize my thoughts on the material you've just read. The fact that I've taken the time to write this material doesn't mean I've got it all figured out. It just means I've taken the time to put my ideas, observations, and learning on paper.

Over the years I have received advice, insight, lessons, and feedback from various people in my life. It is my intent that you are able to also pull some inspiration from what I have shared and apply it to your own life. As I've researched this material over the years one thing that has amazed me is that when I speak with others who might be considered experts in one of the *Eight Facets*, they all thought their area of expertise was certainly the most important.

I believe the facets are all components that make up our life, but *you* must decide what priority you will assign them. Facets like career, finance and health are easier to make goals for improvement because they can be tracked for progress. Is my weight going down, my blood pressure, etc? Is my portfolio increasing or my bank accounts trending upwards? These are tangible things we can easily measure and know if we are making progress, or not.

Aspects like being a better parent, or friend, or getting closer to God in my faith journey aren't so easily defined. These are areas most of us claim to be most important, but we rarely give much thought on how we are doing, let alone improving.

Many times, people talk of having "balance." Don't mistake balance as meaning each of the eight are equal, like trying to balance on a teeter totter. Many people have written about work / life balance suggesting the key is simply to be there, whether at work or away. That's easier said than done. I'm sure we can all relate to a time we've been thinking about work when not there, or any of the other seven while at work. I think a better term is living a life of intentionality.

Intentionality is like being focused with our discretionary time. It's not about quality versus quantity either. It's about making the things that matter be your focus always. As an example, if being a good parent is important then it can't take a backseat to my golf game, or any social media activity, or any time that takes away from my family. I've been entrusted to their upbringing for a brief time. Therefore, it's my responsibility to be there for the formative years as much as possible. I didn't always do that as much as I should have and want to pass along to others that this is a big deal.

Understanding the components of a good marriage doesn't make one. Understanding the principles of money management does not keep you out of debt. Understanding the techniques of a good golf swing does not lower your scores. Understanding the practices of healthy living does not keep you healthy. In the same way understanding the eight facets of life will not necessarily make you have a meaningful and purposeful life. I think a person in one of my early classes hit the nail on the head when he said "all aspects are interdependent of each other. Any can change our attitude in a moment's notice in a positive or negative way."

Knowledge usually isn't our problem; It's action. Too many times we aren't happy with the way things are going but put in as much effort as a kamikaze pilot on his 39th mission. It's like the story of a visitor talking with a friend on his porch. An old dog laying there would moan every so often. When the visitor asked what was wrong with the dog the owner replied, "Oh, he's lying on a nail, but it doesn't hurt bad enough to move."

Could that be said of us? I've heard it said we'll all suffer one of two pains. The pain of discipline, or the pain of regret. Which will you choose? It's about being better. The key is to make small, incremental steps forward day by day. Start by changing the subjects of your daily conversation from the life you are living to the one you desire. Your conversations will lead to opportunities, which will become actions, and thus improvement.

You can't keep saying *I'll get started tomorrow*. Regardless of age or status, if you aren't satisfied with the path, you are on, it's time to rewrite your future.

In the Bible it speaks of two judgements. The first is did you accept Jesus as Lord and Savior? The second is what did you do with the abilities and talents I gave you?

It's your call!

I hope you've found some value in the material. In all *Eight Facets*, I continue to learn and hope to share as I hope you will as well. I've learned more about raising children after mine were gone than I did while they lived with me. Maybe that's normal. Then again, I'd never have learned other options or opinions unless I was learning and open to what has worked for others. I'd encourage you to do the same in all areas of life.

My writings are ninety plus percent mine. However, I'd be the first to admit most of my material comes from reading other books, newsletters, blogs etc. I'm sure I've included material that's been in others work as well. I tried to give credit where credit was due but many times I might not have known where I got the material from. If I liked something, I would save the article but not always the author's name. I say this because I don't want to take credit for anything I didn't do.

I spoke to one writer about borrowing a story he wrote, and he was flattered I enjoyed his work. That's the way I'd like to go through life. With an abundance mindset versus a scarcity mindset.

> *I alone cannot change the world, but I can cast a stone across the water to create many ripples.* Mother Teresa

PHILOSOPHY

I've been a fan of several personal development icons. Probably two of the ones I learned the most from were Zig Ziglar and Jim Rohn who I've mentioned several times throughout my writing. They have both passed away recently but their books and cd's pass along their wisdom for any to read or listen to.

Jim, I recall talking about our philosophy. I understood him to mean it's everything we've allowed into our mind. It's our values we've adopted, and the information we've chosen to believe and act on.

As an example, if I think getting up early and working out or reading or anything else that might jump start my day will have a positive impact on my life that is a part of my personal philosophy.

Likewise, if I see no value in this activity and instead choose to sleep in till noon then I've adopted this as a part of my personal philosophy.

We have the freedom to choose whichever of the above-mentioned examples. However, we accept the consequences as well. If our philosophy was in error, we can't blame anyone else.

The same goes with our eating habits. If I feel like a cheeseburger and fries won't harm me that's a philosophy. The truth is they won't once in a while. However, if we think we can live like that day in and day out I'd suggest we may have a flaw in our philosophy.

The same with our spending habits. If I feel I can start saving tomorrow that is a philosophy I've bought into. I can justify anything I wish to. I deserve it, we deserve it. Why can't we have nice things like the neighbors? I always liked Dave Ramsey's answer to that which is something like, "I will live like no one else now, so I can live like no one else tomorrow."

We have a philosophy about each aspect of the eight facets whether we realize it or not. I'd suggest if parts of your life aren't where you wish they were you'd start by examining and asking some tough questions. When we realize our past decisions got us where we are, that is a monumental step in the right direction. Whether we realize it or not we are taking responsibility for the rest of our lives and that is great news.

Maybe some past decisions weren't the best, but we can learn to make better decisions. In addition, by accepting our past and future we realize our hope is in our hands. We don't have to depend on the government, our relatives, the weather or anything else.

So, a question to ponder is, what have you adopted as your personal philosophy? It's a question you must consider. After all, no decision is still a decision. I hope you won't allow the loudest voice you hear to decide for you.

We each have a tremendous responsibility to give life all we are capable of giving. Many people don't like that task, don't let that be you. You will feel better about yourself and you will influence others more when you live your life to the fullest.

Read all you can, observe all you can, study all you can. Learn from your own experiences as well as other's experiences. Other people's failures are less painful (at least as far as you are concerned) and learning from them will speed your process.

It's not what we get, but what we become, what we contribute, that gives meaning to life.

Philosophy

There is no passion to be found in settling for a life that is less than the one you are capable of living. Nelson Mandela

Everything is Connected

There are two common views of life – the silo view and the connected view. The silo view sees life as a disconnected series of interactions. In the silo view, family and career are separate compartments that don't interconnect. The same can be said for each of the other facets of life.

In the connected view, all of life is intertwined. What happens at home affects work. What happens at church affects home and so on. This view accurately portrays life as it is, messy and tangled. When adults explain their lives this is what they describe:

One last quote from John Wooden to end. There is a choice you have to make in everything you do. So keep in mind that in the end, the choice you make, makes you.

Finish Strong

ABOUT THE AUTHOR

Working over 30 years in a manufacturing environment, Chris was able to learn skills in manufacturing, human resources, accounting, engineering, and purchasing to name a few. Chris was most proud of the fact that moving to different career paths within the organization was always someone else's idea, meaning they sought him out to assist within their department. While this most likely stunted his growth upward in the company, it kept him fresh to take on new challenges and make a difference in the lives of those in which he worked with. He is a husband, father, and grandfather. He and his wife D'Anne survived on one income when that wasn't the norm. In addition, Chris retired comfortably at age 56 due to living a life he outlines in this book. He's taught classes and conducted training both professionally and by volunteering through church, YMCA, and school activities. One of his favorite sayings is, "None of us are as good as all of us." We can learn from everyone. He retired in 2013 and has since been a high school golf coach, junior high basketball coach, volunteered at Kirkmont Center in Logan County, taught Sunday school since 1999, and served as pulpit supply (vacation) for various churches. He also writes weekly columns in a couple of local newspapers. If you'd like to contact him, you may email:theconleys102@gmail.com

www.ingramcontent.com/pod-product-compliance
Lightning Source LLC
LaVergne TN
LVHW011827060526
838200LV00053B/3925